TENNESSEE

DAILY
DEVOTIONS
FOR
DIE-HARD
FANS

VOLUNTEERS

TENNESSEE

Daily Devotions for Die-Hard Fans: Tennessee Volunteers
© 2010 Ed McMinn

Library of Congress Cataloging-in-Publication Data
13 ISBN Digit ISBN: 978-0-9840847-5-3

Manufactured in the United States of America.

For bulk purchases or to request the author for speaking engagements, email contact@extrapointpublishers.com.

Go to http://www.die-hardfans.com for information about other titles in the series.

Cover and interior design by Slynn McMinn.

Every effort has been made to identify copyright holders. Any omissions are wholly unintentional. Extra Point Publishers should be notified in writing immediately for full acknowledgement in future editions.

VOLUNTEERS

To Steve Rodgers
and his family,
True Volunteers for Christ

DAY 1

SOMETHING NEW

Read Colossians 3:1-17.

*"[S]ince you have taken off your old self with its practices
and have put on the new self, which is being renewed in
knowledge in the image of its Creator" (vv. 9-10).*

Something new came to the University of Tennessee on Saturday, Nov. 21, 1891: football.

H.K. Denlinger, who had played football at Princeton in 1890, was hired to direct the athletic program at the local YMCA, and he was the impetus behind the birth of football at UT. By the fall of 1891, he had used his enthusiasm for this newfangled game to generate "sufficient interest among the students and athletic-minded citizens of Knoxville to proceed to form not one team, but two." One of those teams played the first organized football game ever played in Knoxville on Thanksgiving Day 1891 against a team from Harriman.

A second game was scheduled for Saturday with a team from the university taking on a squad from Sewanee in Chattanooga. "The game of football is beginning to obtain a foothold here," the *Knoxville Journal* asserted in a preview of the game. Perhaps fearing the worst, a columnist declared, "If we are routed in this game we will send our baseball team down next spring to balance up accounts."

One would-be player named Honeyman missed out on his chance for history because he had been bitten by a spider. History

VOLUNTEERS

has recorded ten names that made that first road trip, the full-back's identity having been lost for the ages.

Sewanee defeated the Orange and White 24-0. The *Journal* reported -- four days later -- "About one hundred people witnessed the game. . . . After the game all of the boys took in the theater."

Something new had come to Knoxville -- and university life would never be the same again.

New things in our lives do often have a life-changing effect. A new spouse. A new baby. A new job. A new football coach. Even something as mundane as a new television set or lawn mower jolts us with change.

New experiences, new people, and new toys may make our lives new, but they can't make new lives for us. Inside, where it counts – down in the deepest recesses of our soul – we're still the same, no matter how desperately we may wish to change.

A restlessness drives us to seek escape from a life that is a monotonous routine. It's not good enough for someone who is a child of God; it can't even be called living. We want more out of life; something's got to change.

The only hope for a new life lies in becoming a brand new man or woman. And that is possible only through Jesus Christ, he who can make all things new again.

Football is a comparatively new feature of the university, but we have complete confidence in our men and think they will win.
-- Knoxville Journal *on UT's first collegiate football game*

**A brand new you with the promise
of a life worth living is waiting in Jesus Christ.**

DAY 2

YOU NEVER KNOW

Read Matthew 24:36-51.

"No one knows about that day or hour, not even the angels in heaven, nor the Son, but only the Father" (v. 36).

Everyone just knew Peyton Manning would play his college football at Ole Miss. Funny thing about that.

The Ole Miss bloodline in the Manning family is legendary. Dad Archie is the "school's most famous football player, a living legend" who, when Peyton was a high-school senior in 1993, headed up a big fundraising campaign. Mom Olivia was a Rebel homecoming queen. Older brother Cooper made what seemed like the inevitable choice to play in Oxford; "everybody thought [Peyton would] follow the leader to Ole Miss."

Certainly that was what his parents would have liked, but "they decided early that pressure from Mississippi, from family and friends, would not be an influence" on Peyton's decision. That still didn't keep Peyton from getting plenty of calls from Mississippi people. They were definitely counting on him in Oxford.

But Peyton took his usual approach by thoroughly researching both schools. He learned that the Rebs were coming off a 3-5 record in the SEC and that rumors of an NCAA investigation were swirling. In short, they weren't about to make the leap into national prominence. Moreover, Cooper's football career at Ole Miss ended prematurely with a neck and spine condition. Peyton wouldn't be throwing to him. Peyton's research eventually led him to the rich Volunteer tradition, that big stadium, and all those tens of thousands of passionate-to-the-point-of-insanity fans.

When it came time for a decision, Manning told his parents he'd play for Ole Miss if that was what they wanted. UT fans will forever rejoice that they answered, "No, go where your heart tells you to go. He said it was Tennessee."

Just like all the Ole Miss faithful who were so sure about Peyton Manning, we think we've got everything figured out and under control, and then something unexpected happens. About the only thing we can expect from life with any certainty is the unexpected.

God is that way too, suddenly showing up to remind us he's still around. A friend who calls and tells you he's praying for you, a hug from your child or grandchild, a lone lily that blooms in your yard -- unexpected moments when the divine comes crashing into our lives with such clarity that it takes our breath away and brings tears to our eyes.

But why shouldn't God do the unexpected? The only factor limiting what God can do in our lives is the paucity of our own faith. We should expect the unexpected from God, this same deity who caught everyone by surprise by unexpectedly coming to live among us as a man, and who will return when we least expect it.

You pray a lot, and you just know what you're going to do.
— Peyton Manning on his decision to play for Tennessee

God continually does the unexpected,
like showing up as Jesus,
who will return unexpectedly.

DAY 3

TWO FOR THE SHOW

Read Hebrews 11:39-12:2.

"Therefore, since we are surrounded by such a great cloud of witnesses, . . . let us run with perseverance the race marked out for us" (v. 12:1).

Tennessee basketball coach Ray Mears is legendary for both his coaching abilities and the gimmicks he pulled off to put folks into the seats. Before Mears, though, there was John Sines, who once came up with the quite original idea of scheduling two games in one night.

Mears won 278 games in 15 seasons from 1962-77. He coined the phrase "Big Orange Country" and had his team wear bright orange, which nobody did then. "Some of the players thought we looked like a band," he said, but he urged them to have a little pride in their school.

His promotional efforts were part of rebuilding interest in "a dilapidated program" that had been 4-19 in 1961-62. He turned pregame into a sideshow with flashy dribbling routines to "Sweet Georgia Brown." He put 6-5 player Roger Peltz on a unicycle.

Master promoter that he was, though, Mears never did what Sines did on Dec. 1, 1960. Sines preceded Mears as head basketball coach, compiling a 65-81 record over seven seasons. Like Mears, he had to be creative to get people to the old Armory Fieldhouse. Perhaps his most unusual idea was a doubleheader -- two for the price of one - to open the 1960-61 season. He scheduled a

VOLUNTEERS

game against Chattanooga at 7 p.m. and then a nightcap against East Tennessee at 9 "after a few whiffs of oxygen."

The gimmick worked to the extent of drawing a "moderately large" crowd of about 2,500. Led by senior guards Glenn Campbell and Bobby Carter, the Vols won both games.

Like the UT basketball team of 1960, you probably don't have a huge crowd of folks applauding your efforts every day. You certainly don't have TV cameras broadcasting your every move to an enthralled audience. Sometimes you may even feel alone. A child's illness, the slow death of a loved one, financial troubles, worries about your health – you feel isolated.

But a person of faith is never alone, and not just because you're aware of God's presence. You are always surrounded by a crowd of God's most faithful witnesses, those in the present and those from the past. Their faithfulness both encourages and inspires. They, too, have faced the difficult circumstances with which you contend, and they remained faithful and true to God.

With their examples before you, you can endure your trials, looking in hope and faithfulness beyond your immediate troubles to God's glorious future. Your final victory in Christ will be even sweeter because of your struggles.

I did wake up in the middle of the night once and started to call [the two head coaches] to see if they wanted to call it off.
– Coach John Sines, asked if he was apprehensive about the doubleheader

The person of faith is surrounded by a crowd of witnesses whose faithfulness in difficult times inspires us to remain true to God no matter what.

DAY 4

STRANGE BUT TRUE

Read Isaiah 9:2-7.

"The zeal of the Lord Almighty will accomplish this" (v. 7).

Strange as it sounds, Tennessee once had a player kicked out of a football game twice -- in the same game.

The 1950 Vols went 11-1, a prelude to the 1951 national title. They expected to have little trouble with Washington & Lee on Oct. 28. Bert Rechichar returned a punt 100 yards and an interception for 52 yards for a pair of touchdowns, and Jimmy Hahn scored on an 82-yard kickoff return.

Nobody bothered to tell W&L they were supposed to roll over and play dead. They scored two touchdowns in the last quarter and then drove to the Volunteer five in the closing seconds. The Vols held on four downs inside the five to preserve a 27-20 win. UT head coach Bob Neyland said his team was lucky that day.

During the goal-line stand, a fight erupted. One of the referees ordered linebacker/fullback Gordon Polofsky and end Doug Atkins out of the game. Immediately after the ref tossed Polofsky, more commotion broke out, so he didn't have time to escort the Vol to the sideline. Polofsky "moved to the back of the crowd, out of sight," trying to hide among the other players. As play resumed, however, the ref spotted him. So for a second time, he ordered Polofsky to take a seat on the bench.

The source of the ruckus that distracted the referee was Atkins, who refused to leave the field despite the officials' best attempts. At 6-8 and 260 pounds, the mammoth Atkins rarely did much of anything -- on or off the football field -- that he didn't want to.

Tailback Herky Payne recalled that a desperate official finally went over to Neyland and told him to get Atkins "out of here or I'm going to forfeit the game." Neyland replied, "YOU kicked him out; YOU get him off the field."

Life is just strange, isn't it? How else to explain the college bowl situation, Dr. Phil, tattoos, curling, tofu, and teenagers? Isn't it strange that today we have more ways to stay in touch with each other yet are losing the intimacy of personal contact?

And how strange is God's plan to save us? Think a minute about what God did. He could have come roaring down, destroying and blasting everyone whose sinfulness offended him, which, of course, is pretty much all of us. Then he could have brushed off his hands, nodded the divine head, and left a scorched planet in his wake. All in a day's work.

Instead, God came up with a totally novel plan: He would save the world by becoming a human being, letting himself be humiliated, tortured, and killed, and thus establishing a kingdom of justice and righteousness that will last forever.

It's a strange way to save the world – but it's true.

It may sound strange, but many champions are made champions by setbacks.
-- Olympic Champion Bob Richards

**It's strange but true: God allowed himself
to be killed on a cross to save the world.**

BEAUTIFUL PEOPLE

Read Matthew 23:23-28.

"Woe to you, teachers of the law and Pharisees, you hypocrites! You are like whitewashed tombs, which look beautiful on the outside, but on the inside are full of dead men's bones and everything unclean" (v. 27).

Pat Summitt wants her basketball players mean, not pretty. One time, though, she got busted by her players getting pretty herself.

Kristen "Ace" Clement played for the Vols from 1997-2001, a member of the legendary undefeated 1998 national champions as a freshman. She is still among the all-time Vol assist leaders with 427 in her career.

A left-handed point guard, Clement possessed "an almost illusory passing ability." Summitt called her "a sleight-of-hand artist who could make the ball seem to flicker around the court." But Summitt also described Clement as "a glamour girl," "a genuine beauty with lustrous brown hair and brown eyes."

As the 1998 NCAA Tournament neared, to Summitt's dismay, Clement showed up for practice one day with her hair highlighted. Summitt asked her why she did it, and Clement replied. "I wanted to look pretty." That set Summitt off. "We're not here to look *pretty* in March," she retorted. "We're here to look *mean*."

Immediately, though, Summitt knew she had trapped herself. One of her superstitions was to always get her nails and hair done right before a big game. Because she had excoriated Clement, she hesitated this time until her equally superstitious assistant Mickie DeMoss told her she *had* to get her nails done. So she did.

Sure enough, Clement and teammates Semeka Randall and Niya Butts dropped by Summitt's office that day, and Clement spotted the hair and nails. With a sly smile, Clement reminded her coach that in March they were to look mean, not pretty. The players then whooped it up and high-fived at Summitt's expense.

Remember the brunette who sat behind you in history class? Or the blonde in English? And how about that hunk from the next apartment who washes his car every Saturday morning and just forces you to get outside earlier than you really want to?

We do love those beautiful people.

It is worth remembering amid our adulation of superficial beauty that *Vogue* or *People* probably wouldn't have been too enamored of Jesus' looks. Isaiah 53 declares that our savior "had no beauty or majesty to attract us to him, nothing in his appearance that we should desire him."

Though Jesus never urged folks to walk around with body odor and unwashed hair, he did admonish us to avoid being overly concerned with physical beauty, which fades with age despite tucks and Botox. What matters to God is inner beauty, which reveals itself in the practice of justice, mercy, and faith, and which is not only lifelong but eternal.

Ace Clement couldn't sit in the cafeteria without being surrounded by the entire starting backfield of the football team.

-- Pat Summitt

**When it comes to looking good to God,
it's what's inside that counts.**

HOPE CHEST

Read Psalm 42.

"Put your hope in God, for I will yet praise him, my
Savior and my God" (v. 5b).

All the Vols and their fans had was a shred of hope – but that was more than enough.

On the night of Nov. 14, 1998, the 10th-ranked Arkansas Razorbacks had the game in hand against Tennessee in Neyland Stadium. They had the lead and the ball as the clock was running out. For UT, this wouldn't have been just any loss. The Vols were ranked No. 1 in the nation; a defeat here would be brutal and heartbreaking.

Some weak-of-heart Vol fans had given up hope, thinning out the stadium's packed crowd. As a reporter put it, with the game clock under two minutes, Tennessee fans watching on TV were already crying, cursing, praying, and wondering how far their beloved team would fall in the rankings.

The Tennessee players could have lost hope, but they didn't. Instead, they turned their intensity up a notch. Defensive tackle Darwin Walker said the defensive line exploded when the Hogs snapped the ball. "I know the center saw us ready to come," he said. "And it made him jittery. He was almost trying to block before he snapped it. I never saw the line come off the ball so fast." It was too fast for the Arkansas quarterback, who stumbled and fumbled. Defensive tackle Billy Ratliff recovered the ball.

VOLUNTEERS

A rejuvenated offense took the field with 1:43 left and drove 43 yards in five plays. Tailback Travis Henry sailed into the end zone from the one with 28 seconds left to give the Vols their first lead of the night. UT won 28-24. On a night when hope had been stretched pretty thin, hopes for a national championship were renewed.

Only when a life has no hope does it become not worth the living. To hope is not merely to want something; that is desire or wishful thinking. Desire must be coupled with some degree of expectation to produce hope.

Therein lies the great problem. We may wish for a million dollars, relief from our diabetes, world peace, or a way to lose weight while stuffing ourselves with doughnuts and fried chicken. Our hopes, however, must be firmly grounded, or they will inevitably lead us to disappointment, shame, and disaster. In other words, false hopes ruin us.

One of the most basic issues of our lives, therefore, becomes discovering or locating that in which we can place our hope. Where can we find sure promises for a future that we can count on? Where can we place our hope with realistic expectations that we can live securely even though some of the promises we rely on are yet to be delivered?

In God. In God and God alone lies our hope.

You've always got to have a shred of hope.
-- UT Center Spencer Riley after the Arkansas win

God and his sustaining power are the source of the only meaningful hope possible in our lives.

DAY 7

THE SCAPEGOAT

Read Leviticus 16:15-22.

"He is to lay both hands on the head of the live goat and confess over it all the wickedness and rebellion of the Israelites — all their sins — and put them on the goat's head" (v. 21).

Austin Denney looked like the goat in the early going of the 1966 Gator Bowl. Before it was over, though, he was one of the heroes of a Volunteer win.

After moving from fullback before his junior season, Denney "set the modern standard for Tennessee's tight end position with a combination of versatility, speed and fight." As a senior in 1966, he was All-SEC and All-America after he set a school record by catching seven touchdown passes. His nine touchdown catches in his career still stand as the UT record for a tight end. So he undoubtedly wanted to make his last game as a Volunteer a memorable one. It started out that way -- for the wrong reasons.

On New Year's Eve, the Vols met the Syracuse Orangemen in the Gator Bowl. That other orange team featured a memorable backfield tandem of Larry Csonka and Floyd Little. Key to a win for UT, therefore, was minimizing mistakes.

So Denney promptly made a big one on the opening kickoff. He fumbled it and Syracuse recovered. "I think the kicker actually missed the ball and kind of squibbed it," Denney recalled. "I had aspirations of running it back for a touchdown, but I forgot to take the ball." The defense bailed Denney out, though, by holding.

The Vols led 6-0 when coach Doug Dickey called a trick play that completed Denney's transformation from goat to hero. UT lined up for another field goal, but the holder, quarterback Dewey Warren, took the snap and fired the ball into the end zone. Denney went over two Syracuse defenders to haul in the touchdown, and the Vols went on to win 18-12.

A scapegoat could really be useful to have around. Mess up at work? Bring him in to take the heat. Make a decision your children don't like? Let him put up with the whining and complaining. Forget your anniversary? Call him in to grovel and explain.

What a set-up! You don't have to pay the price for your mistakes, your shortcomings, and your failures. You get off scot-free. Exactly the way forgiveness works with Jesus.

Our sins separate us from God because we the unholy can't stand in the presence of the holy God. To remove our guilt, God requires a blood sacrifice. Out of his unimaginable love for us, he provided the sacrifice: his own son. Jesus is the sacrifice made for us; through Jesus and Jesus alone, forgiveness and eternity with God are ours.

It's a bumper sticker, but it's true: We aren't perfect; we're just forgiven.

I never blame myself when I'm not hitting. I just blame the bat, and if it keeps up, I change bats.

— Yogi Berra

For all those times you fail God, you have Jesus to take the guilt and the blame for you.

THOSE THINGS

Read Isaiah 55:6-13.

"For my thoughts are not your thoughts, neither are your ways my ways" (v. 8).

Life was great for Sarah Fekete. She was the best hitter on the best softball team UT had ever had. And then she got hit in the face.

Fekete is one of Tennessee's greatest players. She completed her career in 2006 as a two-time All-America and UT's all-time leader in batting average (.398), on-base percentage, and stolen bases. She is second all-time in runs scored and hits. She set an SEC record in 2006 with 110 hits.

In the middle of her junior season, Fekete was leading all major college players in hitting when one of those things happened. She was hit by a pitch that broke her jaw. Her mouth was wired shut for more than four weeks, and her health suffered. She lost twenty pounds quickly. The injury proved a frustrating one in that the rest of her body was fine, but because she could breathe only through her nose, she couldn't even get her heart rate up.

With her mouth wired shut, her teeth were clinched together and she could communicate only with difficulty. "When people that I know were around me, they thought it was funny at first," she recalled. But she was in constant pain, so "to me it wasn't funny at all."

Fekete finally came back when she was "just healthy enough"

to play, and her season of trauma had a happy ending when the Lady Vols earned their first-ever spot in the College World Series.

She wore a plastic face mask her senior season, led the whole country in hitting with a .500 average, and led the team back into the World Series -- where she was promptly hit in the face again. The mask prevented more injury and another of those things.

You've probably had a few of "those things" in your own life: bad breaks that occur without regard to justice, morality, or fair play. You wonder if everything in life is random with events determined by a chance roll of some cosmic dice. Is there really somebody scripting all this with logic and purpose?

Yes, there is; God is the author of everything.

We know how it all began; we even know how it all will end. It's in God's book. The part we play in God's kingdom, though, is in the middle, and that part is still being revealed. The simple truth is that God's ways are different from ours. After all he's God and we are not. That's why we don't know what's coming our way, and why "those things" catch us by surprise and dismay us when they do occur.

What God asks of us is that we trust him. As the one – and the only one – in charge, he knows everything will be all right for those who follow Jesus.

Sometimes the calls go your way, and sometimes they don't.
-- Olympic Gold Medalist Dr. Dot Richardson

Life confounds us because, while we know
the end and the beginning of God's great story, we
are part of the middle, which God is still writing.

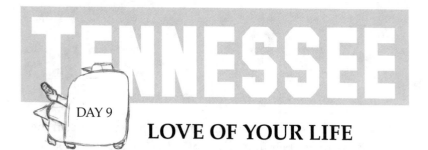

LOVE OF YOUR LIFE

Read 1 John 4:7-21.

"Whoever does not love does not know God, because God is love" (v. 8).

Ole Miss quarterback John Fourcade for years told the story of the time Tennessee defensive end Reggie White sacked him, helped him to his feet, and told him, "God loves you, John."

White is one of the most decorated football players in both UT and NFL history. He played in Knoxville from 1980-83, setting records for most sacks in a career, a season, and a game. His senior season he was All-America and the SEC Player of the Year.

White was known as much for his deep-seated Christian faith as he was for his skills on the gridiron. He once confused UT fans when, after the 5-6 nightmare of 1980, he said he "couldn't change the results, but he could try to be happy and accept what happened as God's will." As if a losing season in Knoxville were God's will!

White loved God deeply early in his life. His grandmother put him in church from the get-go. He said he thought of becoming a minister as early as the eighth grade. He was 17 when he delivered his trial sermon before the congregation and four ministers of his church. He preached on forgiveness and was ordained.

He believed with all his heart that the meek would inherit the earth, but he also knew they wouldn't sack quarterbacks. He was relentless on the field, but he wasn't mean or hurtful. He never taunted opponents. Those who had battled him in a game often kneeled with him in prayer when the game was over.

Membership in the UT chapter of the Fellowship of Christian Athletes grew from ten to 70 while he was its vice president. He frequently stopped students on campus to witness to them, to tell them about the one who was the love of his life.

Your heart rate accelerates, your blood pressure jumps, your mouth runs dry, your vision blurs, and you start stammering. Either you've got the flu or the one you're in love with just walked into the room and smiled at you. Fortunately, if the attraction is based on more than hormones and eye candy, the feverish frenzy that characterizes newfound love matures into a deeper, more meaningful affection. If it didn't, we'd probably die from exhaustion, stroke, heart failure, or a combination thereof.

We pursue true love with a desperation and a ferocity unmatched by any other desire. Ultimately, the Christian life is about that same search, about falling in love and becoming a partner in a deep-seated, satisfying, ever-growing and ever-deepening relationship. The Christian life is about loving so fiercely and so completely that love is not something you're in but something you are. The object of your love is the greatest and most faithful lover of them all: God.

God gave Reggie White an extra-large body so there'd be enough room for his very big heart.

– The Rev. Billy McCool

God is head-over-heels in love with you;
like any lover, he wants you to return the love.

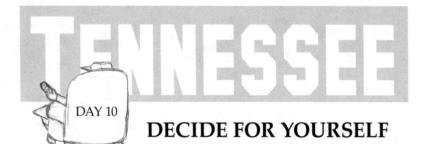

DECIDE FOR YOURSELF

Read John 6:60-69.

*"The words I have spoken to you are spirit and they are
life. Yet there are some of you who do not believe" (vv.
63b-64a).*

The young captain had a decision to make. What he decided
forever changed the fortunes of Tennessee football.

In the spring of 1925, 33-year-old Capt. Robert Reese Neyland
pondered his future as he sat at his desk at the U.S. Military
Academy. His boss, no less an authority than Gen. Douglas
MacArthur, had told Neyland he could become a great soldier.
Interestingly, he "thought he might rather be a football coach."

He knew, though, that to be successful he had to leave the
Academy. He had heard about a couple of jobs that combined
ROTC and football coaching at Iowa and Tennessee. He pulled
down a map and studied the situation logically. Iowa was corn
and cows; there might actually be some people in Tennessee. And,
too, he knew that in Knoxville, the only way to go was up. He
had seen Tennessee play in 1923 in storebought shoes; Army had
waxed them 41-0.

So Neyland decided to investigate the situation at Knoxville.
He made his way south and met Nathan W. Dougherty, a former
All-Southern guard and now an engineering professor and the
faculty chairman of athletics at UT. The two hit it off, and the dean
offered him a job teaching military science and coaching the ends.

VOLUNTEERS

They may well have discussed the fact that the football team had lost five in a row the previous season and the head coach was on the last year of his contract. Neyland decided to take the jobs.

After the 1925 season and a couple of weeks after the fact, Dougherty leisurely announced that Neyland was Tennessee's new head coach. The "real beginning of Tennessee football" was under way. Neyland's record would be 173-31-12 in 21 seasons.

As with Capt. Neyland, the decisions you have made along the way have shaped your life at every pivotal moment. Some decisions you made suddenly and carelessly; some you made carefully and deliberately; some were forced upon you. You may have discovered that some of those spur-of-the-moment decisions have turned out better than your carefully considered ones.

Of all your life's decisions, however, none is more important than one you cannot ignore: What have you done with Jesus? Even in his time, people chose to follow Jesus or to reject him, and nothing has changed; the decision must still be made and nobody can make it for you. Ignoring Jesus won't work either; that is, in fact, a decision, and neither he nor the consequences of your decision will go away.

Carefully considered or spontaneous – how you arrive at a decision for Jesus doesn't matter; all that matters is that you get there.

The best move I ever made.
-- Dean Nathan Dougherty on hiring Bob Neyland

**A decision for Jesus may be spontaneous
or considered; what counts is that you make it.**

DAY 11

JUST IMAGINE

Read Revelation 1:4-18.

"His face was like the sun shining in all its brilliance. When I saw him, I fell at his feet as though dead" (vv. 16b-17a).

Lady Vol basketball without Pat Summitt. The legend with a losing record and nervous before a game. Can you imagine?

The hiring of the winningest coach in the history of college basketball wasn't a sure thing back in 1974. Even Summitt has said that what happened to her was unlikely: "I cannot imagine anyone coming out of college as an undergrad and walking into a job that would allow them to be a head coach at 22."

In 1974, Tennessee's women's basketball program was already successful, posting a 60-18 record in Margaret Hutson's three seasons as head coach. Summitt (then Pat Head) was courted as the graduate assistant. When Hutson took a sabbatical, former coach Nancy Lay, the school's coordinator of women's athletics, assumed that this person she knew as a "marvelous" college player possessed the traits necessary to be a head coach. She recommended Head to Helen B. Watson, the overseer of the PE department, who offered the 21-year-old undergraduate the head coach's job. The fledgling coach actually mulled an offer from Memphis State before she accepted Watson's proposal.

And, yes, she started out 0-1, losing her first game to Mercer University by one point, so Pat Summitt at one time in her career had a losing record. She also started out just like any other rookie coach: nervous. "I was jittery, and I remember that Pat was kind of jittery, too," recalled Diane Brady Fetzer, a senior guard on that 1974-75 team.

Hard to imagine, isn't it?

We are blessed (or cursed) with generally active imaginations. We can, for instance, quite often imagine what someone or some place looks like from a description. We probably have in our minds an image of what Jesus the man looked like.

Some things, however, are beyond our imagining until we experience them or see them in person. Slavery. The birth of our child. Krispy Kreme donuts. Life in prison. Neyland Stadium on game day.

And add to that list the glorified Jesus. When Jesus ascended to Heaven, he assumed his rightful place in glory right there with God the Father, another unimaginable sight. In so doing, Jesus, the gentle man who drew children close to him and wept over the death of a friend, achieved a radiant splendor the likes of which we can't really imagine despite John's attempt to describe the scene for us.

Imagine this: One day we will see the glorified Jesus face to face. What we can't imagine is the depth of the joy we will feel.

When Pat Summitt won her first game as head coach, 53 fans attended and her name wasn't mentioned in the newspaper's game story.
-- Sam Venable, Knoxville News-Sentinel

The glorified Jesus is unimaginable,
as is the joy we will experience
when we come into his presence.

DAY 12

FOOD FOR THOUGHT

Read Genesis 9:1-7.

"Everything that lives and moves will be food for you. Just as I gave you the green plants, I now give you everything" (v. 3).

Growing up, Antone Davis worried every day if he were going to eat the next day. Thus, when he got the chance, he ate as much as he could. And then he showed up at Tennessee.

Davis said, "Manners were not at the top of my list; football was not at the top of my list. Survival was at the top of my list." And that meant food. He spent his senior year of high school at Tennessee Military Institute where he played nose guard. There, "I pretty much got whatever I wanted to eat," Davis recalled. Then came intense recruiting, and Davis continued to wolf down the food. "They weren't going to hassle me with food on recruiting trips," Davis said.

He was recruited by offensive line coach Phillip Fulmer, and the two struck up a relationship. "Coach Fulmer and I were pals," Davis said. "We were buddies. He recruited me, and it was like, 'Where have you been all my life.'" So he committed to Tennessee but took a recruiting visit to South Carolina for the fun of it. While he was in Columbia, he "ate everything I could under the sun."

The inevitable results of that long binge were revealed when Davis arrived in Knoxville in the summer of 1987 to get in shape for camp. When he stepped onto a scale, it groaned in pain; he weighed 349 pounds. Shortly thereafter, Fulmer approached him and asked him how much he weighed. Proud of the weight, Davis replied truthfully. "Three hundred," Fulmer snapped before walking away, leaving Davis wondering where his buddy went.

Two months later when he officially reported, Davis was down to 299 pounds and was on his way to an All-American and NFL career. As a senior in 1990, he won the Jacobs Blocking Trophy as the SEC's best blocker.

Belly up to the buffet, boys and girls, for barbecue, sirloin steak, grilled chicken, and fried catfish with hush puppies and cheese grits. Rachael Ray's a household name; hamburger joints, pizza parlors, and taco stands lurk on every corner; and we have a TV channel devoted exclusively to food. We love our chow.

Food is one of God's really good ideas, but consider the complex divine plan that begins with a seed and ends with French fries. The creator of all life devised a system in which living things are sustained and nourished physically through the sacrifice of other living things in a way similar to what Christ underwent to save us spiritually. Whether it's fast food or home-cooked, everything we eat is a gift from God secured through a divine plan in which some plants and animals have given up their lives.

Pausing to give thanks before we dive in seems the least we can do.

I cut down to six meals a day.
-- Charles Barkley on losing weight

**God created a system that nourishes us
through the sacrifice of other living things;
that's worth a thank-you.**

EXCUSES, EXCUSES

Read Luke 9:57-62.

"Another said, 'I will follow you, Lord; but first let me go back and say good-by to my family'" (v. 61).

Fuad Reveiz became the Miami Dolphins' kicker because he didn't make excuses, something he learned in Knoxville from his college mentor, legendary Vol coach George Cafego.

Many still consider Reveiz to be the greatest placekicker in UT football history. From 1981-84, he was All-SEC three times. He set an NCAA record for percentage of field goals made longer than 40 yards and set UT records for most points scored, field goals made and attempted, and field goal and extra point percentage.

In August 1981, head coach Johnny Majors introduced Reveiz to Cafego, the man whom he called "the most influential man in molding my character" next to his grandfather. Cafego (See Devotion No. 21.) had no experience with Hispanic names, so he asked Reveiz, a native of Colombia, how to pronounce his name, then solved the problem as only the plain-spoken Cafego could do. "I'm not going to study Latin to pronounce your name," he declared. "Your name is Frank." For four years, Cafego would bark, "Frank, let's go" when the time came for Reveiz to kick.

At least until the 1984 Kentucky game, which was Reveiz' last home game. That time, Cafego said, "Fuad, go kick it." "I believe it was his way of saying that I had grown up and earned his respect," Reveiz said.

VOLUNTEERS

One lesson Reveiz learned from Cafego helped launch his pro career in 1985. He was drafted by the Dolphins, who had a veteran kicker on hand. "He was pretty good, but he never missed a field goal in his life," Reveiz said. By that, he meant the kicker always had an excuse. To his surprise, Reveiz got the job. Two years later, Dolphin head man Don Shula told Reveiz he couldn't stand excuse-making, something Reveiz never did, and that helped him make the team.

Has some of your most creative thinking involved excuses for not going in to work? Have you discovered that an unintended benefit of computers is that you can always blame them for the destruction of all your hard work? Don't you manage to stammer or stutter some justification when a state trooper pulls you over? We're usually pretty good at making excuses to cover our failures or to get out of something we don't particularly want to do.

That holds true for our faith life also. The Bible is too hard to understand so I won't read it; the weather's too pretty to be shut up in church; praying in public is embarrassing and I'm not very good at it anyway. The plain truth is, though, that no matter what excuses we make for not following Jesus wholeheartedly, they are not good enough.

Jesus made no excuses to avoid dying for us; we should offer none to avoid living for him.

Coaches don't want to hear about the moon or the stars, or the holder or the snapper.

-- Fuad Reveiz on making excuses

**Try though we might, no excuses can justify
our failure to follow Jesus wholeheartedly.**

DAY 14

THE WALL

Read Philippians 2:1-11.

*". . . that at the name of Jesus every knee should bow, . . .
and every tongue confess that Jesus Christ is Lord" (vv.
10, 11).*

One Tennessee player stood like a wall. "I used my length," said J.P. Prince. In so doing, he preserved what is one of the biggest wins and certainly the most prestigious win in the history of UT men's basketball.

In the semifinals of the Midwest Regional on Friday, March 26, 2010, second-seeded Ohio State hurried down the floor in the closing seconds to tie the game and prevent the Vols from going where they had never gone before. The Tennessee men weren't really expected to be where they were. They were good; they had beaten top-ranked Kansas and second-ranked Kentucky. But a 29-point bludgeoning by those same Wildcats in the semifinals of the SEC Tournament dropped them to a sixth seed.

They made it past 11-seed San Diego State 62-59 and then clubbed 14th-seeded Ohio 83-68. That put Tennessee into the Sweet Sixteen for the sixth time in school history. Never before, though, had the Vols advanced to the Elite Eight.

With 12.9 seconds left, point guard Bobby Maze hit two free throws to give Tennessee a 76-73 lead. Everyone in the place knew the Buckeyes would go to their all-star guard, Evan Turner. Prince had his instructions from the UT coaches: Follow Turner wherever he went. Sure enough, Turner fired a three pointer from the left side but missed. The ball skittered off several hands before it found Turner again. He leaned in for another three-point shot, but this time he met the wall. Prince would not yield, and he blocked the shot. "I'm just glad I had enough left in the tank to make a play at the end," Prince said. "It was a clean block."

And the Vols were on their way to the Elite Eight.

We all build walls. Since we live within ourselves as no one else can, we know our own faults, foibles, and failures intimately. We assume that if people knew the real person inside our skin, they wouldn't like us. Thus, we pose. We put up a false front and hide behind a wall that keeps others from seeing who we really are so we'll appear more acceptable and virtuous to the world.

But it's lonely behind that wall; we hesitate to love and be loved because that means surrender, knocking down the wall and becoming vulnerable. Even when it's Jesus trying to break through, we resist.

But how foolish is that? The purpose of the wall in the first place is to keep others from knowing us, and Jesus already knows absolutely everything there is to know about us. And still he loves us, still he accepts us. To love Jesus isn't surrender; it's victory.

When I finally gave my life over to God, that's when joy and happiness entered my life.

-- NFL Quarterback Kurt Warner

We build walls so others won't know us,
but Jesus knows us already and loves us still,
so why keep him out?

DAY 15

TRUSTWORTHY

Read Psalm 25.

"To you, O lord, I lift up my soul. In you I trust, O my God" (vv. 1-2).

When we're between the lines, we're playing for the person next to us." That declaration by senior receiver Gerald Jones demonstrated the most immediate problem new Volunteer head coach Derek Dooley faced as he began spring practice in 2010: Restoring trust in the coaching staff.

"Coach Dooley could leave next year. You never know." Jones again -- and he should know. "I've had a different coach every year," Jones pointed out. "Three different head coaches and five different position coaches."

On Jan. 15, 2010, Dooley, son of legendary Georgia coach Vince Dooley, was introduced as the Vols' 22nd head football coach. He arrived in the wake of Lane Kiffin's sudden departure from Knoxville after one season as head coach. Dooley's pedigree included three years at Louisiana Tech as head coach and athletic director and a seven-year stint before that as an assistant coach with Nick Saban at LSU and the NFL's Miami Dolphins.

Dooley inherited some of the typical problems a new head coach faces in that he had to find five starting offensive linemen, a running back, and a quarterback. But he faced a unique situation; he found a roster of players who after the recent turmoil and turnover were "more jaded than most 10-year NFL veterans."

VOLUNTEERS

Dooley understood that, noting that the Volunteers "had been through something no other college football player has. With it, there was a tremendous breach in trust." The new coaching staff couldn't, therefore, expect the players to buy into what they said simply because they said it.

Dooley saw a good side to his players' attitude, though. They might not trust the coaches, but they sure trusted each other. He had players who would fight for each other.

The benefits and boons our modern age has given us have come at a price. One of those costs is the erosion of our trusting nature. Once upon a time in America we trusted until we saw a reason not to. Now, wariness is our first response to most situations.

It's not just outlandish claims on TV that have rendered us a nation of skeptics. We've come to accept hucksters as relatively harmless scam artists who are part of living in a capitalistic society. No, the serious damage to our inherent sense of trust has been done in our personal relationships. With much pain, we have learned the truth: Many people just flat can't be trusted.

Ant then there's God, whom we can trust absolutely. He will not let us down; he is incapable of lying to us; he always delivers on his promises; he is always there when we need him.

In God we can trust. It sounds like a motto we might find on a coin, but it's a statement of absolute truth.

Good teams become great ones when the members trust each other enough to surrender the 'me' for the 'we.'
-- NBA Coach Phil Jackson

We look for the scam before surrendering our trust, but we can trust God without hesitation.

THE COMEBACK

Read Acts 9:1-22.

*"All those who heard him were astonished and asked,
'Isn't he the man who raised havoc in Jerusalem among
those who call on this name?'" (v. 21)*

The game was over before most folks had even settled into their seats -- and then the Vols pulled a comeback for the ages.

On Nov. 9, 1991, Tennessee traveled to South Bend to take on Notre Dame. Any Vol fans who made the trip must surely have wished they hadn't once the game got under way. A fumbled punt, an interception return, and a long drive propelled the Irish into a 21-0 lead -- in the first quarter. "I remember wondering if Notre Dame was going to score 80 or 85," said head coach John Majors.

Quarterback Andy Kelly's touchdown pass finally gave the Vols something to cheer about, but the euphoria didn't last long. A Notre Dame field goal and a touchdown off another fumble ran the count to 31-7 in the second quarter. The turning point of the game came with time running out on what is consistently regarded as one of the greatest plays in Tennessee football history. Linebacker Darryl Hardy blocked a Notre Dame field goal, and defensive back Floyd Miley returned it 76 yards for a touchdown. Majors jumped onto a training table at halftime and shouted to his troops, "We're back in this thing."

They were. In the last half, Kelly kept chunking and the defense held Notre Dame to a lone field goal. With nine minutes left to play, UT trailed only 34-28. Dale Carter, a two-time All-American defensive back, then put the Vols in business with an interception at midfield with 5:09 on the clock.

Offensive coordinator Phillip Fulmer anticipated a blitz and made the perfect call. Kelly flipped a screen pass to tailback Aaron Hayden and the play broke for a touchdown. John Becksvoort's extra point completed the comeback at 35-34. The score held up when Notre Dame missed a last-gasp field goal.

Life will have its setbacks whether they result from personal failures or from forces and people beyond your control. Being a Christian and a faithful follower of Jesus Christ doesn't insulate you from getting into deep trouble.

Maybe financial problems suffocated you. A serious illness put you on the sidelines. Or your family was hit with a great tragedy. Life is a series of victories and defeats. Winning isn't about avoiding defeat; it's about getting back up to compete again. It's about making a comeback of your own.

When you avail yourself of God's grace and God's power, your comeback is always greater than your setback. You are never too far behind, and it's never too late in life's game for Jesus to lead you to victory, to turn trouble into triumph. As it was with the Vols against Notre Dame and with Paul, it's not how you start that counts; it's how you finish.

Not in my lifetime and not at Notre Dame.
-- Coach John Majors when asked if he'd ever seen such a comeback

In life, victory is truly a matter of how you finish
and whether you finish with Jesus at your side.

DAY 17

HOMESTAND

Read Joshua 24:14-27.

"Choose for yourselves this day whom you will serve. . . .
But as for me and my household, we will serve the Lord"
(v. 15).

Because of a rule regarding the uniforms basketball teams could wear at home, a tradition was born that makes the uniforms of the Lady Vol basketball team different from that of every other UT team.

In 1968, Joan Cronan became the Lady Vols head coach; she was 23. Not that her young age and relative inexperience would be much of a problem; the program wasn't exactly big-time then. Women's basketball was pretty much a club sport. Jane Hill, one of the pioneers of UT women's basketball, played at a high school so small it has been phased out. Yet she found playing basketball at Tennessee a step down. "College ball was not as serious at that time as high school ball had been," she said.

Cronan had no scholarships and an annual budget of $500. Hill remembers, "We were lucky if we got a crowd of twenty people at our games." Moreover, the Lady Vols didn't even have any uniforms when Cronan took over; they were playing in T-shirts and shorts. Cronan decided to do something about that.

Only a few companies, though, made women's uniforms then, and those that did didn't offer an orange uniform. Cronan found some white uniforms with orange lettering, which was fine for road games. Rules prohibited home teams from wearing white, however, so Cronan had to find some other color. "I had to decide what color went well with orange lettering," she recalled. "I liked Carolina blue," and it was available.

Within a few years, of course, orange uniforms were readily available. By then, however, the Carolina blue had become a unique Lady Volunteer tradition. Look closely at the uniforms next time; you'll see a touch of Carolina blue.

You enter your home to find love, security, and joy. It's the place where your heart feels warmest, your laughter comes easiest, and your life is its richest. It is the center of and the reason for everything you do and everything you are.

How can a home be such a place?

If it is a home where grace is spoken before every meal, it is such a place. If it is a home where the Bible is read, studied, and discussed by the whole family gathered together, it is such a place. If it is a home that serves as a jumping-off point for the whole family to go to church, not just on Sunday morning and not just occasionally, but regularly, it is such a place. If it is a home where the name of God is spoken with reverence and awe and not with disrespect and indifference, it is such a place.

In other words, a house becomes a true home when God is part of the family.

Sure, the home field is an advantage, but so is having a lot of talent.
                                                                -- *Dan Marino*

**A home is full when all the family members –
including God -- are present.**

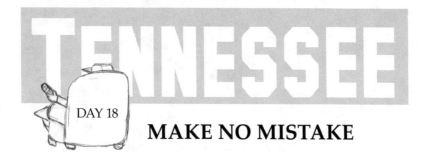

DAY 18

MAKE NO MISTAKE

Read Mark 14:66-72.

"Then Peter remembered the word Jesus had spoken to him: 'Before the rooster crows twice you will disown me three times.' And he broke down and wept" (v. 72).

Making mistakes in a game typically costs a football team. Against South Carolina in 2002, though, a Vols' flub helped them win the game.

The 25th-ranked Volunteers made a bunch of mistakes against the Gamecocks on Nov. 2. "We had some penalties and turnovers we didn't need," asserted center Scott Wells. He was right; the Vols lost two fumbles and committed eight penalties.

Still, Tennessee managed to win 18-10. An early fumble set up a Gamecock field goal. Tennessee answered with an 80-yard scoring drive, highlighted by Jabari Davis' 62-yard romp. Making another mistake with a low snap, the Vols missed the extra point.

Tennessee added two Alex Walls field goals to lead 12-3 in the third quarter before yet another mistake – the second fumble – led to Carolina's lone touchdown. Leading only 12-10, the Vols moved down the field largely behind the running of Cedric Houston. They wound up facing a fourth and one at the Gamecock 5 with 6:25 to play – and made another mistake.

Coach Phillip Fulmer sent the field-goal unit onto the field. But guard Chavis Smith, who had been held up by a trainer attending to an injury, didn't realize that line coach Mike Barry had already sent out a sub. He rushed onto the field where tackle Will Ofenheusle wisely counted twelve helmets and sprinted off the field. The Vols needed a time out.

That gave the coaches time to talk it over, and they decided to go for it. Quarterback Casey Clausen used a block by Jason Witten to roll right and score. Proving they could still make mistakes, the Vols missed the extra point.

It's distressing but it's true: Like football teams and Simon Peter, we all make mistakes. Only one perfect man ever walked on this earth, and no one of us is he. Some mistakes are just dumb. Like locking yourself out of your car or falling into a swimming pool with your clothes on. Other mistakes are more significant. Like heading down a path to addiction. Committing a crime. Walking out on a spouse and the children.

All these mistakes, however, from the momentarily annoying to the life-altering tragic, share one aspect: They can all be forgiven in Christ. Other folks may not forgive us; we may not even forgive ourselves. But God will forgive us when we call upon him in Jesus' name.

Thus, the one fatal mistake we can make is ignoring the fact that we will die one day and subsequently ignoring the fact that Jesus is the only way to shun Hell and enter Heaven. We absolutely must get this one right.

It looked like a Chinese fire drill.
-- Coach Mike Barry on the confusion that led to the Vols' last TD

Only one mistake we make sends us to Hell
after we die: ignoring Jesus while we live.

A LONG SHOT

Read Matthew 9:9-13.

"[Jesus] saw a man named Matthew sitting at the tax collector's booth. 'Follow me,' he told him, and Matthew got up and followed him" (v. 9).

Polio. Rheumatic fever. Smallest kid on the block. Quit the team once. Kicked off it another time. And this guy would be a star? Talk about your basic long shot.

When he was nine, Frank Emanuel contracted rheumatic fever. At 10, he got a touch of polio that for a while left him unable to move his left leg. He was the smallest kid in his class. In fact, he almost didn't get to a class at all. His father decreed that young Frank was needed on the farm, so he picked cotton as a six-year-old. Only when he was eight did he start school after intervention from local authorities.

Emanuel needed only two weeks in Knoxville to get so homesick he decided to give up football and get a job. When he walked into his house, UT Coaches Ralph Chancey and Skeeter Bailey were waiting for him. They talked him into coming back.

Emanuel played both ways in 1963, but Coach Doug Dickey arrived and changes were afoot. Emanuel ran afoul of Dickey's tightened discipline when he got into "a spectacular neighborhood brawl" and was kicked off the team.

With no money and no resources, he lived under the stadium; teammates smuggled him food from the dining hall. Dickey

VOLUNTEERS

eventually gave him a second chance as long as he stayed out of trouble. Emanuel did. In the 19-3 win over Kentucky in 1965, he had what may well be the most spectacular game any Tennessee linebacker has ever had. He made 26 tackles, 17 unassisted, and made four straight stops near the goal with the score tied in the third quarter. He intercepted a pass that led to a touchdown.

Frank Emanuel the long shot was All-America in 1965 and was eventually elected to the College Football Hall of Fame.

Matthew the tax collector was another long shot, an unlikely person to be a confidant of the Son of God. We may not get all warm and fuzzy about the IRS, but our government's revenue agents are nothing like Matthew and his ilk. He bought a franchise, paying the Roman Empire for the privilege of extorting, bullying, and stealing everything he could from his own people. Tax collectors of the time were "despicable, vile, unprincipled scoundrels."

And yet, Jesus said only two words to this lowlife: "Follow me." Jesus knew that this long shot would make an excellent disciple.

It's the same with us. While we may not be quite as vile as Matthew was, none of us can stand before God with our hands clean and our hearts pure. We are all impossibly long shots to enter God's Heaven. That is, until we do what Matthew did: get up and follow Jesus.

Overcoming challenges should never be considered a long shot.
-- Mother of disabled child on MightyMikeBasketball.com

**Only through Jesus does our status change
from being long shots to enter God's Kingdom
to being heavy favorites.**

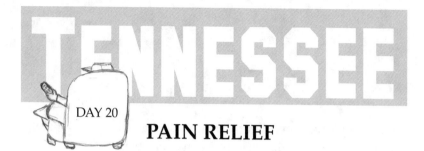

DAY 20

PAIN RELIEF

Read 2 Corinthians 1:3-7.

"Just as the sufferings of Christ flow over into our lives, so also through Christ our comfort overflows" (v. 5).

Whatever else you can say about Bridgette Gordon, you have to admit she could play with pain.

Gordon is one of the most decorated players in UT women's basketball history. In 1990, her No. 30 was retired, the second Lady Vol jersey to be so honored. She played in Knoxville from 1985-89, leading the team to four straight Final Fours and two national championships. She was the first freshman ever to lead UT in scoring and was twice All-America. She finished her career as the all-time leading scorer in NCAA tournament history.

She was not, however, having her best game on April 2, 1989, in the national championship game against Auburn, and Pat Summitt took notice. She called a time out to talk to her team and saw that Gordon "was only half listening to me. She was glazed. . . . She had her hand over her mouth." Summitt knew she had to get to her star somehow. "She was our leading scorer, our go-to player. We needed her to take over the game."

So Summitt got right in Gordon's face, ignoring the other four players and snapped, "What's wrong with you?" When Gordon said nothing, Summitt ordered her, "Get your hand away from your mouth and get back in there and *do* something."

Gordon nodded that she understood the message. She then

went back onto the floor and sank three straight shots, keying a UT outburst that sent the Vols up by 18 and on their way to the school's second national championship. She finished with 27 points and 11 rebounds.

After the game, Summitt learned that right before the time out in which she had so chastised Gordon, her star had taken an elbow to the face with such power that a tooth had been knocked loose. She wound up needing a root canal to save it.

Nothing, though, not even Gordon's pain, could save Auburn.

Since you live on Earth and not in Heaven, you are forced to play with pain. Whether it's a car wreck that left you shattered, the end of a relationship that left you battered, or a loved one's death that left you tattered -- pain finds you and challenges you to keep going.

While God's word teaches that you will reap what you sow, life also teaches that pain and hardship are not necessarily the result of personal failure. Pain in fact can be one of the tools God uses to mold your character and change your life.

What are you to do when you are hit full-speed by the awful pain that seems to choke the very will to live out of you? Where is your consolation, your comfort, and your help?

In almighty God, whose love will never fail. When life knocks you to your knees, you're closer to God than ever before.

That showed me Bridgette had it in her heart.
-- Senior Guard Melissa McCray on Gordon's play after being hit

When life hits you with pain, you can always turn to God for comfort, consolation, and hope.

MIRACLE PLAY

Read Matthew 12:38-42.

"He answered, 'A wicked and adulterous generation asks for a miraculous sign!'" (v. 39)

On a sunny summer day in 1936 in a "near-nothing" town in West Virginia, a miracle happened that changed a life.

Or at least George Cafego always called it a miracle when Bob Neyland showed up at a baseball field to look at a "rag-tag infielder who played tailback in the fall." "When you come from where I did, when you're looking at living and dying in the coal mines, the best thing that ever happened to me was when General Neyland said, 'I'll take care of you,'" Cafego said. What Neyland meant was a scholarship.

Cafego certainly needed one because he had nothing. His parents were dead, and for a while he moved in with a married sister, "but times got so rough, she couldn't afford to feed and clothe me." So he bounced around, living with high-school coaches, with miners in a boarding house, and "wherever I could find a corner to sleep."

He had six dollars and a borrowed suitcase held together with string when he got on a bus for Knoxville. After he eventually located the athletic department and was directed to a dormitory, he had no sheets or blankets because nobody told him to bring any. Even if they had, he wouldn't have had them. When Neyland decreed that his players should wear a suit to away games, one of the coaches took Cafego to town and "bought me the first suit and tie I ever owned."

Tennessee got a handsome return on its investment. Cafego became an All-American running back who was elected to the College Football Hall of Fame. After his pro career was cut short by knee injuries, he eventually wound up back in Knoxville as an assistant coach. He coached for thirty years until 1985.

Miracles -- like the sudden appearance of someone who changes your life -- defy rational explanation. Or escaping with minor abrasions from an accident that totals your car -- that's a miracle. So is recovering from an illness that seemed terminal. Underlying the notion of miracles is that they are rare instances of direct divine intervention that reveal God.

But life shows us quite the contrary, that miracles are anything but rare. Since God made the world and everything in it, everything around you is miraculous. Even you are a miracle. Your life thus can be mundane, dull, and ordinary, or it can be spent in a glorious attitude of childlike wonder and awe. It depends on whether or not you see the world through the eyes of faith. Only through faith can you discern the hand of God in any event; only through faith can you see the miraculous and thus see God.

Jesus knew that miracles don't produce faith, but rather faith produces miracles.

Do you believe in miracles? Yes!
– Al Michaels when U.S. beat USSR in hockey in 1980 Winter Games

Miracles are all around us,
but it takes the eyes of faith to see them.

DAY 22

THE GREATEST

Read Mark 9:33-37.

"If anyone wants to be first, he must be the very last, and the servant of all" (v. 35).

Vols head coach Johnny Majors, only four years removed from a national championship at Pittsburgh, called what he had just seen "the greatest performance by any team of mine, any time, any place." And nobody, especially the Auburn Tigers, who were the victims, saw it coming.

On Sept. 27, 1980, the Tennessee Volunteers had a day that most football teams can only wish for. What the largest home crowd ever to witness an Auburn game saw was the worst home-field defeat in the school's long gridiron history. Tennessee thrashed the Tigers 42-0.

The 1-2 Vols entered the game as an underdog. Moreover, Tennessee was unsettled at quarterback. Before the team left for Auburn, Majors announced that Jeff Olszewski would be the starting quarterback in place of Steve Alatorre. Olszewki was regarded as the better runner with Alatorre considered the better passer. But Olszewski came out firing, at one stretch completing eleven straight passes. "As I recall, it was a mediocre day for me passing, and a great day for our receivers," Olszewski said. He recalled hitting an Auburn linebacker right in the chest with his first pass. "He could have gone up the sideline for a touchdown."

But he didn't. Instead, Reggie Harper, Anthony Hancock, and

the other Vol receivers caught practically everything Olszewski threw their way. The running game was equally dominating. James Berry scored three touchdowns, and Terry Daniels ran for 125 yards. The defense forced six turnovers and held highly touted James Brooks to 36 yards.

UT led 28-0 by halftime. Auburn coach Doug Barfield said he felt like "General Custer among all these Indians." Overall, it was one of Tennessee's greatest games ever, one for the ages.

We all want to be the greatest. The goal for the Volunteers and their fans every season is the national championship. The competition at work is to be the most productive sales person on the staff or the Teacher of the Year. In other words, we define being the greatest in terms of the struggle for personal success. It's nothing new; the disciples saw greatness in the same way.

As Jesus illustrated, though, greatness in the Kingdom of God has nothing to do with the world's understanding of success. Rather, the greatest are those who channel their ambition toward the furtherance of Christ's kingdom through love and service, rather than their own advancement, which is a complete reversal of status and values as the world sees them.

After all, who could be greater than the person who has Jesus for a brother and God for a father? And that's every one of us.

We had some confidence we could win, but not anything like that.
-- Jeff Olszewski

**To be great for God has nothing to do
with personal advancement and everything to do
with the advancement of Christ's kingdom.**

DOOR PRIZE

Read Revelation 3:14-22.

"Here I am! I stand at the door and knock. If anyone hears my voice and opens the door, I will come in" (v. 20).

While Lady Vol fans today are accustomed to legitimate shots at national championships, there was a time when the team only perched on the doorstep and knocked on the championship door. Then in 1987, they blew the door off its hinges.

In seven trips to the Final Four, the Lady Vols had never won it all. They had not been ranked No. 1 in ten years. On Dec. 14, 1986, the Lady Vols whipped top-ranked and defending national champion Texas 85-78 behind sophomore Bridgette Gordon, who scored 26 points. UT was No. 1.

They didn't stay there, coming out of the SEC Tournament at No. 8 with a 23-6 record. Moreover, they were second fiddle to Auburn, which beat the Lady Vols twice. UT beat Tennessee Tech and Virginia in the NCAA Tournament, only to face those same second-ranked Auburn Tigers again. In perhaps their best game of the season, the Lady Vols blasted Auburn 77-61 behind 33 points from Gordon and 15 points and 13 rebounds from center Sheila Frost. "If we play the way we played tonight, we'll bring home a national championship," Gordon said.

They drew No. 4 Long Beach State in the semifinals. History records that the most lasting aspect of the game was a comment by a State forward, who, when comparing the two teams, called the Vols "corn-fed chicks." The phrase has stuck with the team that gave Tennessee its first championship.

UT won 74-64 in yet another upset of a titan, leaving only one left: third-ranked Louisiana Tech. The Lady Vols buried the Lady Techsters 67-44. They didn't just open the door; they kicked it down. "Tennessee's corn-fed chicks had come home to roost" -- with a national championship.

You're all settled down in your favorite chair; your spouse is somewhere in the house; the kids are doing their homework or texting. It's calm and quiet.

And then someone knocks on the front door. The dog erupts into a barking frenzy. Your spouse calls, "Can you get that?" You tell the kids to answer the door, whereupon they whine in unison, "I'm busy."

So you abandon your chair. A stranger, a friend, or a Girl Scout with cookies -- it makes no difference. You open the door.

How ironic and heartbreaking it is that so many people who willingly open the doors of their homes when anybody knocks keep the doors of their hearts shut when Jesus knocks. That's what Jesus does; he knocks at the door of your heart like a polite and unassuming guest. He'll step inside only if you invite him, but he's the one visitor above all others you want to let in.

Tennessee had a stigma. We were the perennial bridesmaid, never the bride. I couldn't stand it.
-- Pat Summitt on the program prior to the 1986-87 season

Jesus won't barge into your heart; he will enter only when you open the door and invite him in.

DAY 24

HUGS AND KISSES

Read John 15:5-17.

"Now remain in my love" (v. 9b).

Sarah Wyche hugged her boy, Bubba, many times, but one embrace in particular had to be among the best ever.

Most of the recruiters backed away after Joseph Murry "Bubba" Wyche, Jr., tore his knee up before his senior year of high school. Tennessee stayed. Then two weeks into spring practice of his sophomore season of 1965, Wyche's knee buckled, requiring more surgery. He was redshirted. In 1966, he passed six times for 18 yards and ran the ball three times, losing eight yards.

In 1967, Wyche's best shot was at being Dewey Warren's backup. The time lost to an appendectomy bumped him behind Charlie Fulton. But Warren got hurt, and then Fulton went down early in the Georgia Tech game. Wyche was in, having never even taken a snap from All-American center Bob Johnson. He threw two touchdown passes to Richmond Flowers, UT won 24-13, and he was named the Southeastern Back of the Week.

All that got him was Alabama in Birmingham the next week. Tennessee won again 24-13, snapping the Tide's streak of 26 games without a loss. In his first start, Wyche hit eight of 14 passes and rushed for twelve yards.

Wyche's parents had missed the Tech game because he saw no chance of playing, so he sold the tickets for some extra spending money. The Alabama game was a sellout, so his mother didn't have a ticket. Still she went to Birmingham and trekked from gate to gate, trying to get in. Finally, she opened her wallet, showed a gatekeeper her driver's license, and pleaded, "My boy is starting at quarterback for Tennessee. I've got to get in." The sympathetic gatekeeper waved her in with the warning, "You'll have to stand if you can't find a seat."

That didn't matter. She was there and saw it all. When the game was over, she found Bubba and gave him one great big hug.

That friend from college you haven't seen for a while. Your family, including that aunt with the body odor. We hug them all, whether in greeting, in good-bye, or simply as a spontaneous display of affection. The act of physically clutching someone tightly to us symbolizes how closely we hold them in our hearts.

So whether you are a profligate hugger or a more judicious dispenser of your hugs, a hug is an act of intimacy. Given that, the ultimate hugger is almighty God, who, through Christ, continuously seeks to draw us closer to him in love. A good hug, though, takes two, so what God seeks from us is to hug him back.

We do that by keeping him close in our hearts, by witnessing for his Son through both words and deeds. To live our lives for Jesus is to engage in one long, refreshing heartwarming hug with God.

It was one sweet embrace.
-- Chris Cawood on Sarah Wyche's hugging Bubba after the Bama game

**A daily walk with Christ means we are so close
to God that we are engaged in one long,
joyous hug with the divine.**

DAY 25

DREAM WORLD

Read Joel 2:26-28.

"Your old men will dream dreams, your young men will see visions" (v. 28).

Bill Bates was positive his lifelong dream of playing for the Dallas Cowboys was about to come true. At least he would be playing in the NFL. And then he didn't get drafted.

Bates was a four-year starting safety for the Vols from 1979-82. He was named second-team All-SEC both his junior and senior seasons. An eternal optimist, Bates never doubted that he could make it in the pros. He had long dreamed of being a Dallas Cowboy because his high-school uniform was a close match to the silver and blue outfits the Cowboys sported.

The NFL draft in 1983 consisted of two days of six rounds each. "I was pretty pumped up about my chances," Bates said. When the first day went by without his being drafted, he was unperturbed. His dreams came crashing down, though, when he wasn't drafted on the second day either. He determined NFL scouts had decided he was too slow to play pro ball.

The next day, Bates was thinking about getting a real job when the phone rang. A man from the Dallas Cowboys told Bates he would have been their selection on the thirteenth round and offered him a free-agent contract. Bates jumped at the chance.

His dream was about to come true! Well, maybe not. At the Cowboys' camp, he noticed busloads of guys, 185 football players in fact. "Imagine -- 185 guys who thought they had been drafted in the thirteenth round," Bates said. If that wasn't deflating enough, he learned that the man who had signed him worked in the equipment room.

But Bates' dream did come true. He spent fifteen seasons with the Cowboys, made All-Pro, and played in two Super Bowls.

You have dreams. Maybe to make a lot of money. Write the great American novel. Or have the fairy-tale romance. But dreams often are crushed beneath the weight of everyday living; reality, not dreams, comes to occupy your time, attention, and effort. You've come to understand that achieving your dreams requires a combination of persistence, timing, and providence.

But what if your dreams don't come true because they're not good enough? That is, they're based on the alluring but totally unreliable promises of the world rather than the true promises of God, which are a sure thing.

God calls us to great achievements because God's dreams for us are greater than our dreams for ourselves. Such greatness occurs, though, only when our dreams and God's will for our lives are the same. Your dreams should be worthy of your best – and worthy of God's involvement in making them come true.

An athlete cannot run with money in his pocket. He must run with hope in his heart and dreams in his head.
-- Olympic Gold Medalist Emil Zatopek

Dreams based on the world's promises
are often crushed; those based on God's promises
are a sure thing.

DAY 26

THE PIONEER SPIRIT

Read Luke 5:1-11.

"So they pulled their boats up on shore, left everything and followed him" (v. 11).

Coach [Ray] Mears never talked to me about it and I never talked to him about it. It was just coach and player." But when it turned into player and player, Larry Robinson became a trailblazer for UT basketball.

"It" was the white elephant in the room in 1971. When Robinson joined the team, he became UT's first African-American basketball player. "I didn't live in a vacuum," Robinson said. "I was aware of what the situation was. . . . I felt if I could be a good citizen, everything would be fine, that I could help the societal situation."

Robinson was, in fact, the perfect man for his time and his pioneering situation. Both his academics and his character were impeccable. He was one of 15 children raised in a Christian home in Virginia. He was such a good athlete that football coach Bill Battle offered him a football scholarship; he eventually played on the Dallas Cowboys' taxi squad for two seasons.

The football team had integrated in 1968, so Robinson wasn't the only black athlete on campus. But Mears and his assistants took a decidedly low-key approach to Robinson's groundbreaking role. Lloyd Richardson, who was Robinson's roommate for the 1971-72 season said that race "just never entered the mix. He was accepted whole-heartedly, and that's a credit to him. He was a joy

VOLUNTEERS

to be around."

Robinson averaged 10.2 points and a team-high nine rebounds that first season as the Vols went 19-6 and tied Kentucky for first place in the SEC. As a senior in 1972-73, Robinson was a pioneer again when he was named team captain. He averaged 11.7 points and 8.5 boards to lead the Vols to a second-place SEC finish.

Going to a place in your life you've never been before requires a willingness to take risks and face uncertainty head-on. You may have never helped change the history of a program at a major college, but you've had your moments when your latent pioneer spirit manifested itself. That time you changed careers, ran a marathon, volunteered at a homeless shelter, learned Spanish, or went back to school.

While attempting new things invariably begets apprehension, the truth is that when life becomes too comfortable and too familiar, it gets boring. The same is true of God, who is downright dangerous because he calls us to be anything but comfortable as we serve him. He summons us to continually blaze new trails in our faith life, to follow him no matter what. Stepping out on faith is risky all right, but the reward is a life of accomplishment, adventure, and joy that cannot be equaled anywhere else.

When I decided to come to Tennessee, as far as black or white or red or yellow, we were a team.

-- Larry Robinson

Unsafe and downright dangerous, God calls us out of the place where we are comfortable to a life of adventure and trailblazing in his name.

THE PIONEER SPIRIT 53

DAY 27

THE INTERVIEW

Read Romans 14: 1-12.

*"We will all stand before God's judgment seat. . . . So
then, each of us will give an account of himself to God"*
(vv. 10, 12).

Heath Shuler's first interview for the college scouts took place,
quite naturally, on the football field. It was a fiasco

In 1993, Shuler was the SEC's Player of the Year. The Vols went
9-2-1 as he threw for 25 touchdowns, led the SEC in passing, and
finished sixth in the nation. He was runner-up for the Heisman
Trophy and in 2009 was honored as an SEC Legend.

Shuler played his high-school football at a small school in
Western North Carolina, but the college scouts still found him. At
one stretch, recruiters invaded the family home for sixty consecutive evenings. Most of them were like UT offensive coordinator
Phillip Fulmer, who watched a few minutes of Shuler on film and
declared, "That's the one."

The circus really started, though, in 1990 with the opening
football game of Shuler's senior year. This was the first time
the recruiters could watch Shuler play in person. His on-the-job
interview didn't exactly go the way he would have planned it.

It was raining when the head coach told his squad to bring
both their practice and their game uniforms to the game so they
could warm up in their practice clothes, change, and look good
for the game. Shuler forget his game pants and had to coerce a

reserve into giving him his.

When he took the field in the other boy's pants, Shuler discovered that the opposition was determined not to let him beat them. On defense, they deployed ten defensive backs. So, instead of passing, he repeatedly tucked the ball and took off. "I ran for about a hundred and fifty yards that night," Shuler said.

All those coaches in the stands didn't really get to see what they came for. Still, Heath Shuler's interview was a success.

You know all about job interviews even if you've never had one on a football field. You've experienced the stress, the anxiety, the helpless feeling. You tried to appear calm and relaxed, struggling to come up with reasonably original answers to banal questions and to cover up the fact that you thought the interviewer was a total geek. You told yourself that if they turned you down, it was their loss, not yours.

You won't be so indifferent, though, about your last interview: the one with God. A day will come when we will all stand before God to account for ourselves. It is to God and God alone – not our friends, not our parents, not society in general – that we must give a final and complete account.

Since all eternity will be at stake, it sure would help to have a surefire reference with you. One – and only one -- is available: Jesus Christ.

I hereby apply for the head coaching job at Auburn.
-- Shug Jordan's complete job application in 1951

You will have one last interview
-- with God -- and you sure want Jesus
there with you as a character witness.

HURRY UP AND WAIT

Read Acts 1:1-1:14.

"Do not leave Jerusalem, but wait for the gift my Father promised, which you have heard me speak about" (v. 4).

The Vols got a long lesson in waiting when they played Ole Miss in 2004.

Television's imperial command moved the kickoff from the afternoon to 8 p.m. Oxford time, or 9 p.m. Knoxville time. "When people are going to bed in Knoxville, we'll still be playing," remarked Vol punter Dustin Colquitt about the late start, which left UT's players and coaches with a lot of time to kill. A lot of time to sit around in the team hotel and watch TV and wait, listen to music and wait, or sleep and wait.

"I hate the late start," declared running backs coach Trooper Taylor. "The day takes forever. You sit there looking at the clock all day." Offensive lineman Rob Smith simply tried to make the best out of the long day; he slept a lot. "I'm a big sleeper," Smith said. "I sleep all day when we're not having meetings."

Many of the players and coaches hunted for a football game to watch on TV. Not Colquitt. He never watched football before a game. "I've been flipping through the channels before and have seen a punt get blocked . . . and then I start thinking, 'Oh, man, that's horrible for that guy.' I just don't want to see that stuff," he said.

After the long wait, the Vols of 2004 continued their march to the SEC championship game and the Cotton Bowl with a 21-17 win. UT trailed 17-14 in the fourth quarter when freshman Erik Ainge hit Robert Meachem for a 39-yard gain and then found Bret Smith two plays later for a game-winning 30-yard touchdown.

The long wait was over.

You rush to your doctor's appointment and wind up sitting in the appropriately named waiting room for an hour. You wait in the concessions line at a Vol game. You're put on hold when you call a tragically misnamed "customer service" center. All of that waiting is time in which we seem to do nothing but feel the precious minutes of our life ticking away.

Sometimes we even wait for God. We have needs, and we desperately call upon the Lord and are disappointed when we perhaps get no immediate answer.

But Jesus' last command to his disciples was to wait. Moreover, the entire of our Christian life is spent in an attitude of waiting for Jesus' return. While we wait for God, we hold steadfast to his promises, we continue our ministry, we remain in communion with him through prayer and devotion.

In other words, we don't just wait; we grow stronger in our faith. Waiting for God is never time lost.

I don't like it because you have to sit around and twiddle your thumbs all day.
    -- UT Offensive Line Coach Jimmy Ray Stephens on the late start

**Since God acts on his time and not ours,
we often must wait for him,
using the time to strengthen our faith.**

UNBELIEVABLE

Read Hebrews 3:7-19.

"See to it, brothers, that none of you has a sinful, unbelieving heart that turns away from the living God" (v. 12).

The Lady Vols in January were in "near collapse." Even a rival coach sought to console Pat Summitt by telling her to "hang in there till next year." And then they did what not even the most faithful of their fans must have believed was possible: They won the national championship.

As December and January of 1996-97 unrolled, the defending national champions were a mess. At one stretch, they lost five of eight, including the worst home loss in ten years, to fall to 10-6.

When Summitt received the above-mentioned affirmation from UNC's Sylvia Hatchell, she realized almost everybody had written her team off. HBO had, cancelling a documentary because the Lady Vols weren't winning. Summitt and her coaches "hung in with their own private belief" in this team, "though barely so. The temptation to look ahead . . . was overwhelming but in the end resisted. 'We couldn't focus on next year,' said assistant coach Mickie DeMoss. 'It wouldn't be fair to these kids.'"

They finished 23-10 and fifth in the SEC, the worst season in 11 years. But they had two weeks to prepare for the NCAA tourney, and they were ready. They were more intense and more aggressive. They whipped Grambling, Oregon, and Colorado and then upset UConn 91-81 in the regional finals. The Huskies had not lost as many games in five years as the Vols had that season.

They entered the Final Four with the worst record of any team in history. And yet, the Lady Vols won their fifth national title, beating Notre Dame and Old Dominion.

Who would have believed it?

What we claim not to believe in reveals much about us. UFOs. Global warming. Sasquatch. Aluminum baseball bats and the designated hitter. Most of what passes for our unbelief has little effect on our lives. Does it matter that we don't believe a Ginsu knife can stay sharp after repeatedly slicing through tin cans? Or that any other team besides Tennessee is worth pulling for?

That's not the case, however, when Jesus and God are part of the mix. Quite unbelievably, we often hear people blithely assert they don't believe in God. Or brazenly declare they believe in God but don't believe Jesus was anything but a good man and a great teacher.

At this point, unbelief becomes dangerous because God doesn't fool around with scoffers. He locks them out of the Promised Land, which isn't a country in the Middle East but Heaven itself.

Given that scenario, it's downright unbelievable that anyone would not believe.

If you had asked me about a possible national championship after we played Old Dominion [on Jan. 7], I'd have said you're crazy.
-- Senior Forward Abby Conklin

Perhaps nothing is as unbelievable as that some people insist on not believing in God or his son.

DAY 30

DEAD WRONG

Read Matthew 26:14-16; 27:1-10.

"When Judas, who had betrayed him, saw that Jesus was condemned, he was seized with remorse" (v. 27:3).

Son, you're not good enough to play major-college ball." "He can't play defense or offense." Boy, were they wrong.

The player being denigrated so badly was Tim Irwin. He grew up in Knoxville, and as he tried to pick a college, he sent a football film to Notre Dame, "being a good Catholic kid and all." What he got for his trouble was a succinct note from Irish head coach Dan Devine saying Irwin did not have major-college potential.

Nevertheless, Tennessee recruited him, and he was there when new head coach Johnny Majors arrived in 1977. He recalled that the coaches' perception of Tennessee football "was not good, and they were pretty much trying to eliminate who was there." That included Irwin, who had had serious shoulder surgery and been redshirted. "It was hang-on time right then," he said.

Coach Jim Dyer, who became steadfast friends with Irwin, said that the tackle's name came up one day at a staff meeting. They asked Dyer if Irwin could play defense for him. Dyer bluntly replied, "Not only can he not play defense, but he can't play offense, either."

Irwin was determined to prove both his own coaches and the Notre Dame coaches wrong. He knew he wasn't the best athlete around, but the "one thing I knew, though, was that I could try and outwork everybody else."

His first start came in a loss to Notre Dame in 1978. In 1979, however, the Vols blasted the Irish 40-18. A Notre Dame lineman said, "That No. 78 [Irwin] is as good as anybody I will see all year long." Tim Irwin had proved Dan Devine wrong, and he proved his own coaches wrong by making All-SEC in 1980 and going on to a 14-year career in the NFL.

There's wrong, there's dead wrong, and there's Judas wrong. We've all been wrong in our lives, but we can at least honestly ease our conscience by telling ourselves we'll never be as wrong as Judas was. A close examination of Judas' actions, however, reveals that we can indeed replicate in our own lives the mistake Judas made that drove him to suicidal despair.

Judas ultimately regretted his betrayal of our Lord, but his sorrow and remorse, however boundless, could not save him. His attempt to undo his initial wrong was futile because he tried to fix everything himself rather than turning to God in repentance and begging for mercy.

While we can't literally betray Jesus to his enemies as Judas did, we can match Judas' failure in our own lives by not turning to God in Jesus' name and asking for forgiveness for our sins. In that case, we ultimately will be as dead wrong as Judas was.

Inside of a ring or out, ain't nothing wrong with going down. It's staying down that's wrong.

-- Muhammad Ali

**A sin is the first wrong; failing to ask God
for forgiveness of it is the second.**

DAY 31

IN THE KNOW

Read John 4:19-26, 39-42.

"They said to the woman, . . . 'Now we have heard for ourselves, and we know that this man really is the Savior of the world'" (v. 42).

Because the Vol defense knew something, they pulled off one of the most famous plays in Volunteer history and preserved the school's greatest gridiron upset.

The Vols of 1959 managed only a 5-4-1 record and were big underdogs when LSU pulled into town on Nov. 7. The Tigers were undefeated and were ranked No. 1. They had won the national championship in 1958, had won nineteen straight, and hadn't given up a touchdown in thirty-eight quarters.

A run by Heisman-Trophy winner Billy Cannon gave LSU a 7-0 lead that appeared to be enough since Tennessee managed only 38 yards offense the first half. For the Tigers, it wasn't enough, though. They tried a pass in the third quarter, and UT's Jim Cartwright intercepted it, followed blocks by Mike LaSorsa and Cotton Letner, and went 59 yards to tie the game.

LSU promptly fumbled after the kickoff at its 29. UT completed its only pass of the day before fullback Neyle Sollee rumbled into the end zone. Tennessee led 14-7, but the Tigers were far from finished. They scored with 13:44 to play and went for two to take the lead. The two-point conversion was so new that Tennessee had neither attempted one nor defended one. Everyone knew

VOLUNTEERS

Cannon would get the call, but the key was which side he would run on.

The Volunteers knew. As Vol defensive lineman Wayne Grubb recalled, "We knew from the films that when they ran the sweep to their right, Cannon would move back a bit. . . . I saw this happen." He called the defense accordingly, and when Cannon indeed swept right, the defense was there to pull off what became known in Volunteer lore as "The Stop." Grubb tripped Cannon up, and defensive backs Charles Severance and Bill Majors came up quickly to finish the stop short of the goal line. UT won 14-13.

The Tiger defense just knew. You also know some things in your life for certain. That your spouse loves you, for instance. That you are good at your job. That tea should be iced and sweetened. That a bad day fishing is still better than a good day at work. That the best barbecue comes from a pig. You know these things even though no mathematician or philosopher can prove any of this on paper.

It's the same way with faith in Jesus: You just know that he is God's son and the savior of the world. You know it in the same way that you know Tennessee is the only team worth pulling for: with every fiber of your being, with all your heart, your mind, and your soul. You just know, and because you know him, Jesus knows you. And that is all you really need to know.

We knew everything that LSU would do.

-- Charles Severance

**A life of faith is lived in certainty and conviction:
You just know you know.**

DAY 32

HOMEBODIES

Read 2 Corinthians 5:1-10.

"We . . . would prefer to be away from the body and at home with the Lord" (v. 8).

Most Tennessee football players can simply take a quick trip home to see the family when they get a little homesick. Not Constantin Ritzmann, though; his home was in Germany.

Ritzmann was born in Freiburg, Germany. When he was 14, his older brother began playing American football with a small club. "It was just a bunch of guys with no coach," he remembered. "They just bought uniforms and started hitting each other." The younger Ritzmann tagged along to the practices for three years until his family moved to Berlin where he began playing serious football for the first time.

Before long, Ritzmann dreamed of playing football in America. When he was picked for an NFL program that exposes promising athletes to American football, his dream came to fruition. He played a year of high-school ball in Tallahassee that drew the attention of recruiters. He picked UT largely because that was where his childhood idol, Reggie White, had played.

"Physically, he had a lot of ground to make up because he hadn't had the exposure to the weight room," Vol Coach Phillip Fulmer said about Ritzmann. He agreed. "Fundamentally, I had no idea how to play the game," Ritzmann said. One advantage he had was blazing speed for a man who stood 6-4 and weighed 240

VOLUNTEERS

pounds; he actually was a track sprinter.

Ritzmann eventually became a starting defensive end for the Vols as a junior in 2002. In 2003, he was a team captain. The Buffalo Bills signed him as an undrafted free agent in 2004, and in 2005 with the Atlanta Falcons, he became the first German-born non-kicker to play in an NFL game.

Despite the distance from home, Ritzmann adapted easily to America. When he had a good game, he would tell his parents to order a copy of it from a European company. They would see it about a month after the game occurred.

Home is not necessarily a matter of geography. It may be that place you share with your spouse and your children, whether it's Germany or Tennessee You may feel at home when you return to Knoxville, wondering why you were so eager to leave in the first place. Maybe the home you grew up in still feels like an old shoe, a little worn but comfortable and inviting.

God planted that sense of home in us because he is a God of place, and our place is with him. Thus, we may live a few blocks away from our parents and grandparents or we may relocate every few years, but we will still sometimes feel as though we don't really belong no matter where we are. We don't; our true home is with God in the place Jesus has gone ahead to prepare for us. We are homebodies and we are perpetually homesick.

Everybody's better at home.

— Basketball Player Justin Dentmon

**We are continually homesick for our real home,
which is with God in Heaven.**

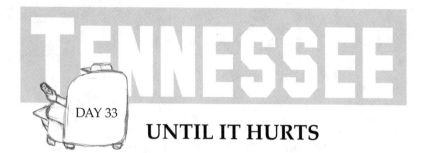

UNTIL IT HURTS

Read 1 Peter 4:12-19.

*"Rejoice that you participate in the sufferings of Christ,
so that you may be overjoyed when his glory is revealed"
(v. 13).*

Rejoice in your sufferings. That Bible-based philosophy served to inspire one of the greatest Lady Vols of them all.

After leading Tennessee to two straight national titles, Candace Parker turned pro following the 2007-08 season. She may still be best known for being the first woman to dunk in an NCAA Tournament game and to dunk twice in a game.

Parker was a three-time All-America. In 2008, she won the Naismith Award as the top women's player in the country. She won the John R. Wooden Award in both 2007 and 2008 as the country's most outstanding women's player. She set Lady Vol career records for free throws made and blocked shots and is second all-time in career rebounding average, third in career points, and fourth in career scoring average (19.4).

That Parker had a year of eligibility remaining after the 2007-08 season illustrates why Romans 5:3 is the foundation of the belief system that drives and shapes her. The verse instructs us to rejoice in our sufferings because they produce perseverance, character, and hope. Candace Parker knows a little bit about suffering and physical pain.

In the summer of 2003 before her senior year of high school, she tore an ACL when she came down for a rebound. After surgery and intensive rehab, she was playing again months before the doctors said she would be able to. But when Parker arrived in Knoxville in 2004, her knee was swollen. She had more surgery that basically rebuilt the knee, and she missed the entire season, receiving a medical redshirt. To remind her that there will always be tough times, she wears "PCH" on her wrist when she plays: the perseverance, character, and hope of Romans 5:3.

Unlike Candace Parker, we don't usually include actual physical pain and suffering as part of the price we are willing to pay to succeed. We'll work overtime, we may neglect our family, we may even work ourselves into exhaustion, but actual pain and suffering that may even lapse into agony? They are definitely not part of our job description. What would we give up to avoid pain and suffering in our daily lives? Everything?

Jesus faced just such a decision. Merely by choosing to, he could have easily evaded the horrific pain and suffering he underwent. Instead, he opted for his love for you over his own well-being, and agony was part of his decision for love.

Now we all face the question: How far do we go with Jesus? Do we bail out on him when it gets inconvenient? Or do we walk with him all the way even when it hurts – just as Jesus did for us?

There are times when we suffer and go through adversity, but God puts adversity there, and we can do it.

-- *Candace Parker*

We must decide whether we'll walk all the way with Jesus, even when it hurts, or whether we'll bail out when faith gets inconvenient.

DAY 34

TIME FOR A CHANGE

Read Romans 6:1-14.

"Just as Christ was raised from the dead through the glory of the Father, we too may live a new life" (v. 4).

You would think a football coach who adopted his offense from other coaches and who insisted that the kicking game ruled would never introduce significant changes to the game. In Gen. Robert Neyland's case, you would be wrong.

Neyland unquestionably is one of college football's greatest coaches ever. From 1926 through 1952 -- with interruptions for military assignments in 1935 and from 1941-45 -- he oversaw a virtual dynasty in Knoxville, winning 82.9 percent of all his games. He lost only 31 times in 21 years as head coach.

But Neyland coached in an age when football was played much more conservatively than it is today. He ran a single-wing offense that he frankly borrowed from some of the other great coaches of the 1920s. He based his approach to the game on several principles that included "One good blocker is worth three ball carriers"; "No offensive play is used in a game until it has been rehearsed 500 times"; and "The kicking game rules."

Such a staunch advocate of conservative football would hardly be expected to initiate far-reaching changes in the game. But Neyland did. For instance, he was the first coach in the South to use press box telephones to the field. He was the first coach to use game films for evaluation, tearaway jerseys, low-top shoes, and

VOLUNTEERS

canvas coverings to protect the field from the weather.

He was one of the first coaches to house his players in motels the night before a game to minimize distractions. He had his own personal weatherman and, if the forecast was for rain, would have his team practice with muddy, even soapy, footballs. Anticipating the emphasis of today's game on the stopwatch, he timed how long it took his punters and passers to release the ball.

Gen. Neyland not only won, but he changed the game too.

Anyone who asserts no change is needed in his or her life isn't paying attention. Every life has doubt, worry, fear, failure, frustration, unfulfilled dreams, and unsuccessful relationships in some combination. The memory and consequences of our past often haunt and trouble us.

Recognizing the need for change in our lives, though, doesn't mean the changes that will bring about hope, joy, peace, and fulfillment will occur. We need some power greater than ourselves or we wouldn't be where we are.

So where can we turn to? Where lies the hope for a changed life? It lies in an encounter with he who is the Lord of all Hope: Jesus Christ. For a life turned over to Jesus, change is inevitable. With Jesus in charge, the old self with its painful and destructive ways of thinking, feeling, loving, and living is transformed.

A changed life is always only a talk with Jesus away.

Change is an essential element of sports, as it is of life.
-- Erik Brady, USA Today

**In Jesus lie the hope and the power
that change lives.**

THE GOOD FIGHT

Read 1 Corinthians 10:1-6.

"Though we live in the world, we do not wage war as the world does. The weapons we fight with are not the weapons of the world" (vv. 3-4a).

When he was at Tennessee, Steve Kiner was not exactly a peace-loving man.

Kiner was one of the most dominating linebackers in Volunteer history. A three-year starter, he was All-SEC and All-America in both 1968 and '69. He was the SEC Defensive Player of the Year in 1969 and was elected to the College Football Hall of Fame in 1999.

His reputation for brawling preceded him to Knoxville, and he certainly embellished it. A scout squad player once tried to chop-block him in practice; Kiner broke his jaw with one punch. "To this day, I feel badly about that one," he once said.

After a young player rolled up Kiner's legs in practice, Kiner grabbed his face mask, lifted his helmet, and popped him in the nose. The enraged player went to the training room and returned with two scalpels, determined to cut Kiner's throat. Kiner told the player to put the weapons down before he got seriously injured. When the player persisted, Kiner clobbered him.

One night in the athletic dorm dining room, a rather large basketball player squeezed in at a table, telling Kiner that if he didn't like the tight spacing to move. "I thought he was joking," Kiner said, "but I looked him right in the eye and decided he wasn't." The basketball player proceeded to announce that he could whip Kiner and pushed him. Kiner promptly slugged him, picked him up, and slammed him onto the table. End of fight. In what many regarded as a miscarriage of justice, Kiner was told not to come back into the dining room.

Generally, violence is not the Christian way, though in Kiner's defense he eventually earned three degrees and became a model citizen and mental health therapist. Following Jesus' admonition to turn the other cheek has rendered many a Christian meek and mild in the name of obedience. But we need to remember that the Lord we follow once bullwhipped a bunch of folks who turned God's temple into a flea market.

With Christianity in America under attack as never before, we must stand up for and fight for our faith. Who else is there to stand up for Jesus if not you? Our pretty little planet -- including our nation -- is a battleground between good and evil. We are far from helpless in this fight because God has provided us with a powerful set of weapons. Prayer, faith, hope, love, the Word of God itself and the Holy Spirit -- these are the weapons at our command with which to vanquish evil and godlessness.

We are called by God to use them, to fight the good fight, not just in our own lives but in our nation and in our world.

It wasn't a good idea to take on Kiner.

-- UT Coach Lon Herzbrun

**'Stand up, Stand up for Jesus' is not
an antiquated hymn but is a contemporary call
to battle for our Lord.**

DAY 36

CROWD CONTROL

Read Matthew 27:15-26.

"When Pilate saw that he could do nothing, but rather that a riot was beginning, he took some water and washed his hands before the crowd" (v. 24 NRSV).

The unruly crowd kept the first-ever Tennessee-Alabama game from getting the legendary series off to a grand start.

On Nov. 28, 1901, in Birmingham, the two played to an unsatisfactory 6-6 tie in "a game that began with every prospect of a splendid struggle but ended up in an unpleasant controversy." "It was anything but an enjoyable game," wrote the *Birmingham News.*

The problem wasn't the players or their effort, but rather the crowd. They kept running onto the field, getting in the players' way, and refusing to leave. "After almost every down the spectators would rush across the side lines and form a compact ring around the struggling teams, preventing beyond a possibility any further play."

A local police squad tried its best to keep the crowd under control, but they "were of little avail against the curiosity of the majority of the enthusiasts." Every time the spectators rushed onto the field, a lengthy time out resulted as officials shooed them away to create enough space for the players to continue.

Then ten minutes into the last half, the two teams got into a heated dispute over an offside call against Alabama. Naturally,

VOLUNTEERS

most of the crowd immediately rushed onto the field to have a voice in the discussion. Alabama refused to play any further unless the decision were reversed.

This delay plus the innumerable holdups occasioned by the uncontrollable crowd all combined to stretch the game to such lengths that darkness began to fall. Thus, the game was called, and an unsatisfactory 6-6 tie initiated one of the nation's greatest football rivalries.

Teenagers seem to catch particular grief about going along with the crowd. Adults, too, often behave in ways contrary to what their conscience tells them is right simply because they fear the disapproval of the people they're with at the time.

So they chuckle at a racial joke. Make fun of a coworker nobody likes. Drink too much and stay out too late. Remain silent when God is cursed. It remains true, though: Just because the crowd does it doesn't make it right. Even Pontius Pilate understood that.

The followers of Jesus Christ are called to separate themselves from the crowd by being disciples. That is, we give to Jesus nothing less than everything we are and everything we have. Jesus is the top priority in a disciple's life, and everything else – everything else – stands behind Jesus. A disciple never goes along with the crowd; he goes along with Jesus.

Almost every football game played in Birmingham in late years ha[s] been marred by the inability of the managers to handle the crowd.
-- Birmingham News *after the 1901 UT-Alabama game*

Just because everybody's doing it doesn't make it right, especially in the way you follow Jesus.

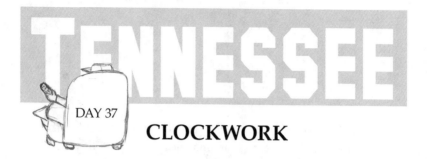

CLOCKWORK

Read Matthew 25:1-13.

"Keep watch, because you do not know the day or the hour" (v. 13).

The UT men's basketball team made history on the night of Dec. 15, 1973 with a game the likes of which will never be seen again -- thank goodness. The Volunteers played the lowest-scoring game of the modern era.

Only one night after they scored 96 points in a win over DePaul, the Vols beat Temple 11-6 in a game in which neither team made a field goal the last half. Temple coach Don Casey saw the DePaul game and knew his team couldn't run with the Vols. So in this era long before the institution of the shot clock prior to the 1985-86 season, Casey told his team to use up as much time as possible with each possession. On the other hand, UT coach Ray Mears didn't like the way his team matched up against Temple in a man-to-man defense, so he packed the Vols in tight with a zone.

The result was a standoff, and neither coach would budge. UT point guard Rodney Woods remembered that teammate Austin Clark "kind of ventured out a few times" to put some pressure on the Owls, but the coaches "threaten[ed] to kill him if he didn't get back and keep things tight."

Freshman Ernie Grunfeld scored to put Tennessee ahead 7-5 with 12:44 left in the first half. Temple stalled the rest of the half before committing a turnover right before the horn sounded. John

Snow hit a technical free throw with 17:58 to play to run the score to 8-5. Temple then held the ball until only about two minutes remained. Snow hit three more free throws in the final seconds, and Temple got a free throw at the end.

Seventeen total points. Needless to say, nobody enjoyed the game. Disgruntled, annoyed, and bored Tennessee fans pelted the court with ice. After the game, UT President Ed Boling asked Mears to bring the players back out for a scrimmage to at least give the fans something to watch. Mears obliged and used the game for years to lobby for a shot clock.

We may pride ourselves on our time management, but the truth is that we don't manage time; it manages us. Hurried and harried, we live by schedules that seem to have too much what and too little when. By setting the bedside alarm at night, we even let the clock determine how much down time we get. A life of leisure actually means one in which time is of no importance.

Every second of our life – all the time we have – is a gift from God, who dreamed up time in the first place. We would do well, therefore, to consider what God considers to be good time management. After all, Jesus himself warned us against misman-aging the time we have. From God's point of view, using our time wisely means being prepared at every moment for Jesus' return, which will occur -- well, only time will tell when.

It was so tight and nerve-wracking because every point was important.
– Rodney Woods on the 1973 Temple game

We mismanage our time when we fail
to prepare for Jesus' return even though
we don't know when that will be.

DAY 38

WEATHERPROOFED

Read Nahum 1:3-9.

"His way is in the whirlwind and the storm, and clouds are the dust of his feet" (v. 3b).

Tennessee and Kentucky met in 1950 in what may well be the worst conditions in Volunteer football history. It was so cold that every time center Bob Davis spit blood after an injury, it would hit his face guard and turn into an icicle.

"It makes me cold to think about it." So spoke Davis almost fifty years after the game of Nov. 25, 1950, when ninth-ranked UT hosted third-ranked Kentucky. The Vols had practiced under beautiful sunny skies on Thanksgiving, but snow started falling that night and kept falling all day Friday. A storm brought a half foot of snow and plunging temperatures.

Shields-Watkins Field was covered with a tarp; a small army of fraternity boys and other volunteers gamely shoveled off the snow. "They had to chop and dig and it ruined the $10,000 tarp," remembered Davis. "That was a lot of money in those days." The manpower wasn't on hand to shovel the seats, so the 45,000 extremely hardy fans who braved the 13-degree temperatures had to make do as best they could.

As if the brutal cold weren't bad enough, both Davis and future All-American fullback Andy Kozar had their noses broken. When Davis leaned over the ball, blood dropped onto it, which naturally led to some complaints from another future All-America, running back Hank Lauricella. So in the last half, Davis wore a face guard for the first and only time, resulting in the icicles.

While the field was playable, the deplorable conditions made handling the ball virtually impossible. Kentucky lost eight fumbles and several interceptions; UT fumbled seven times. Davis fell on one of the Wildcat fumbles to set up a 28-yard TD pass from Lauricella to Bert Rechichar for the game's only score.

A thunderstorm washes away your golf game or the picnic with the kids. Lightning knocks out the electricity just as you settle in at the computer. A tornado interrupts your Sunday dinner and sends everyone scurrying to the hallway. A hurricane cancels your beach trip.

For all our technology and our knowledge, we are still at the mercy of the weather, able only to get a little more advance warning than in the past. The weather answers only to God. Snow and bone-chilling cold will be totally inconsiderate of something as important as a Volunteer football game.

We stand mute before the awesome power of the weather, but we should be even more awestruck at the power of the one who controls it, a power beyond our imagining. Neither, however, can we imagine the depths of God's love for us, a love that drove him to die on a cross for us.

I'd come from Pennsylvania, so I had played in a lot of cold games in high school, but that took the cake.
-- Andy Kozar on the 1950 Kentucky game

The power of the one who controls the weather
is beyond anything we can imagine,
but so is his love for us.

DAY 39

JUST OLD-FASHIONED

Read Leviticus 18:1-5.

*"You must obey my laws and be careful to follow my
decrees. I am the Lord your God" (v. 4).*

Women students at the University of Tennessee should engage
in physical education "to strengthen weak ankles and increase
their lung capacity." My, how attitudes have changed.

Today, we cannot comprehend the University of Tennessee's
athletic program without the Lady Vols. We are accustomed to
cheering for them and being dazzled by their grace, strength,
ability, and commitment. In an earlier age, though, a different,
old-fashioned attitude prevailed as evidenced by UT's 1899
curriculum that included the bit about ankles and lungs.

Contrary to what many Lady Vol fans may believe, the women
athletes of UT began competition in the early 1900s. Basketball
was the first women's varsity sport, a step removed from the times
only a few years before when "socially acceptable physical activities for women included croquet, archery, and tennis." Those
pioneer women played basketball against the likes of Carson-
Newman College and the University of Chattanooga.

On March 16, 1920, women students asked the university for a
single athletic association that would include both genders and
would present varsity letters to female athletes. Their request,
interestingly enough, was granted. The women's varsity competition expanded to include track, swimming, and tennis.

VOLUNTEERS

In the late 1920s, the old-fashioned perception of women in sports rose up again. UT educators denounced intercollegiate sports as elitist. Women's varsity basketball was eliminated after the 1926 season, and the other sports soon followed, available only at the intramural level until a volleyball tournament in 1959.

Usually when we refer to some person, some idea, or some institution as old-fashioned, we are delivering a full-fledged insult (with the exception, of course, of ice cream and candy). They're out of step with the times and the mores, hopelessly out of date, totally irrelevant, and quite useless.

For the people of God, however, "old-fashioned" is exactly the lifestyle we should pursue. The throwbacks are the ones who value honor, dignity, sacrifice, and steadfastness, who can be counted on to tell the truth and to do what they say. Old-fashioned folks shape their lives according to eternal values and truths, the ones handed down by almighty God.

These ancient laws and decrees are still relevant to contemporary life because they direct us to a lifestyle of holiness and righteousness that serves us well every single day. Such a way of living allows us to escape the ultimately hopeless life to which so many have doomed themselves in the name of being modern.

Hippity-hus! Hippity Hus! What in the Thunder's the matter with us? Nothing at all! Nothing at all! We are the girls who play basket ball!
-- Rather old-fashioned cheer in 1906 UT yearbook

The ancient lifestyle God calls us to still directs us to a life of contentment, peace, and joy, which never grows old-fashioned.

BODY LANGUAGE

Read 1 Corinthians 6:12-20.

"Do you not know that your body is a temple of the Holy Spirit, who is in you, whom you have received from God? . . . Honor God with your body" (vv. 19, 20b).

He sure didn't look like much of a football player, once being described as looking like "Friar Tuck in a high school production of *Robin Hood*." Round body and all, though, he was one of UT's greatest linemen ever.

Herman Hickman was 5-10 and weighed 213 pounds when he showed up to play football for Tennessee in 1928. As an adult, he managed to shrink to 5-9 1/2 and balloon to 330 pounds. He was a starting guard for UT as a 17-year-old sophomore.

When he was a senior in 1931, the Vols played a charity game at Yankee Stadium against New York University. UT won 13-0. NYU's most serious threat came with a first down at the Tennessee five. Four Hickman plays later, NYU had managed to back up to the 18. The NYU coach wanted to know if "the little fat man from Tennessee was all that tough." The player replied, "I'll tell you how tough he was. He kept calling me a yankee, and I pretended I didn't hear him."

Legendary journalist Grantland Rice went back to his office after the game and changed his All-American team to add Hickman to it. Years later, Rice said Hickman was the best guard the South ever produced. UT coach Bob Neyland replied that Hick-

VOLUNTEERS

man was the best guard *college football* had ever produced.

After an All-Pro football career and a successful stint as a wrestler, Hickman eventually became head football coach at Yale and was on the first staff at *Sports Illustrated*. When he picked Georgia Tech to beat UT in 1956 and the Vols won, the flamboyant round man who consumed a lot of food in his life literally ate his words, a headline reading, "Hickman Picks Tech."

Your body may never be as round as Herman Hickman's was, but most of us still don't see a body beautiful when we look into a mirror. Too heavy, too short, too pale, too gray, and where'd all the hair go? We often compare ourselves to an impossible standard Hollywood and fashion magazines have created, and we are inevitably disappointed.

God must have been quite partial to your body, though, because he personally fashioned it and gave it to you free of charge. Your body, like everything else in your life, is thus a gift from God. But God didn't stop there. He then quite voluntarily chose to inhabit your body, sharing it with you in the person of the Holy Spirit. What an act of consummate ungratefulness it is then to abuse your God-given body by violating God's standards for living. To do so is in fact to dishonor God.

I can usually tell after the first steak or two if a dinner is going to be up to par.

-- Herman Hickman

You may not have a fine opinion of your body,
but God thought enough of it
to personally create it for you.

DAY 41

FACING THE MUSIC

Read Psalm 98.

"Sing to the Lord a new song, for he has done marvelous things" (v. 1).

Come on Dewey, hum that tater." The Swamp Rat had his linemen singing.

Dewey Warren grew up in the marshes around Savannah. Once he was late for practice and his coach, former Vol Lamar Leachman, asked if he had been "swimming, boating, or just slopping around in a swamp buggy." He then told the sophomore he was just like an old swamp rat. The nickname stuck.

Tennessee did their former player a favor by taking Warren, even though he "was slow as smoke." He played linebacker as a freshman in 1963. He was redshirted in 1964. By the spring, he was No. 2 on the depth chart behind Charley Fulton.

When Fulton was injured against Ole Miss, "Warren jogged onto the field as if he belonged," and immediately the whole hurdle burst out laughing. "You are," was the reply to the obvious question. Warren didn't have his helmet.

That game was to be Tennessee's introduction to its passing game as the Swamp Rat went on to become the school's first pure passing quarterback. The blocking schemes weren't designed for anything remotely resembling a passing attack, so Warren was knocked around pretty good that day. After the game, he was limping around, and a coach asked if he'd be able to play the next week. He replied, "As long as I can stand on one leg and raise my right arm, Old Dewey will be humming that tater."

The linemen picked up on the comment and set it to music. They soon had a huddle song, "Come on Dewey, hum that tater."

The Swamp Rat hummed it all right. Before he finished in 1967, he set practically every school passing record worth mentioning, including yards, completions, attempts, and touchdowns for a career. His 1716 yards and 18 touchdowns in 1966 were also school records.

Maybe you can't play a lick or carry a tune in the proverbial bucket. Or perhaps you do know your way around a guitar or a keyboard and can sing "Rocky Top" or "Come on Dewey, Hum That Tater" on karaoke night without closing the joint down.

Unless you're a professional musician, however, how well you play or sing really doesn't matter. What counts is that you have music in your heart and sometimes you have to turn it loose.

Worshipping God has always included music in some form. That same boisterous and musical enthusiasm you exhibit when the Vols score a touchdown should be a part of the joy you have in your personal worship of God.

When you consider that God loves you, he always will, and he has arranged through Jesus for you to spend eternity with him, how can that song God put in your heart not burst forth?

I like it because it plays old music.
-- Pitcher Tug McGraw on his '54 Buick

You call it music; others may call it noise;
God calls it praise.

DAY 42

KEEP OUT!

Read Exodus 26:31-35; 30:1-10.

"The curtain will separate the Holy Place from the Most Holy Place" (v. 26:33).

One of Tennessee's greatest basketball players ever started playing the game because he didn't want to be an outsider.

Ernie Grunfeld is a Volunteer legend. From 1973-77, after being recruited by about two hundred colleges, he displayed his considerable talents in Knoxville and terrorized SEC opposition. He paired with Bernard King to form the "Ernie and Bernie Show" and left as UT's all-time leading scorer with 2,249 points; he was subsequently bumped to No. 2 by Allan Houston in 1993. Grunfeld also has the second-best scoring average in Tennessee history at 22.3 points per game, behind King. In 2008, his number 22 was retired, only the second Volunteer to be accorded that honor. (King was the first.)

Grunfeld was born of Jewish parents in Romania. His family fled to America to escape religious persecution with Ernie was 9. He remembered that he was saddened when friends wept at the airport, but "he was all smiles when the plane landed in New York City." He can still recall the exact arrival time.

The family settled in Forest Hills, a New York City suburb. The first chore facing a 9-year-old Jewish kid from Eastern Europe was to find some way to fit into his new culture. For Ernie, that way turned out to be basketball.

VOLUNTEERS

He naturally found his way onto the local playgrounds; he got his hands on a basketball for the first time when he was 10. "I wanted to belong in a new neighborhood," he said, "and I found out fast if you wanted to belong you'd better play basketball."

So he did. Only he played it better than everybody else. The kid looking to belong became the ultimate insider, a college star and two-time All-America.

That civic club with membership by invitation only. The bleachers where you sit while others frolic in the sky boxes. That neighborhood you can't afford a house in. You know all about being shut out of some club, some group, some place. "Exclusive" is the word that keeps you out.

The Hebrew people, too, knew about being told to keep out; only the priests could come into the presence of the holy and survive. Then along came Jesus to kick that barrier down and give us direct access to God.

In the process, though, Jesus created another exclusive club; its members are his followers, Christians, those who believe he is the Son of God and the savior of the world. This club, though, extends a membership invitation to everyone in the whole wide world; no one is excluded. Whether you're in or out depends on your response to Jesus, not on arbitrary gatekeepers.

There are clubs you can't belong to, neighborhoods you can't live in, schools you can't get into, but the roads are always open.
                                                              -- Nike

Christianity is an exclusive club, but an invitation is extended to everyone and no one is denied entry.

ANGER MANAGEMENT

Read James 1:19-27.

"Everyone should be quick to listen, slow to speak and slow to become angry, for man's anger does not bring about the righteous life that God desires" (vv. 19-20).

Kevin Burnett's anger was taking him down the wrong path until his mother shocked him with a dramatic demonstration of where he was headed.

Linebacker Burnett had an All-SEC senior season for the Vols in 2004 and was drafted into the NFL. He and Michael Munoz were Tennessee's first junior captains since 1944. "Kevin exemplifies excellence," teammate Mark Jones once said. Burnett won the Go Vols Award for community service in 2003 after he logged more than 150 hours of charity work.

But once upon a time, when he was a child, Burnett's anger almost got the best of him. The catalyst was the death of his father in a car wreck. Burnett was 5. "He was very angry about his father's death," his mother said. He stole, he set things on fire, he hit people. "I had no conscience, no conscience at all," Burnett said about that troubled time. "I remember the time I stole something and got caught. I was no older than 7. The store didn't catch me. My mom did. She beat the mess out of me."

The nadir of his rebellion and anger came when his mother and he argued and he hit her. He was 9 and he was too big for her to restrain him in a physical confrontation. His mother acted. She told him to pack a bag and took him down to Los Angeles' 77th Precinct. There she told the desk sergeant that Kevin had hit her. "Take him back there and let him see what happens when you hit your mother," she instructed the sergeant. As she left, she saw the sergeant handcuff her son to a bench. After an hour, she went back and found Kevin in tears. "I never want to do this again," he said. He never did.

Our society today is well aware of anger's destructive power because too many of us don't manage our anger as Kevin Burnett ultimately did. Anger is a healthy component of a functional human being until – like other normal emotions such as fear, grief, and worry – it escalates out of control. Anger abounds when UT loses; the trouble comes when that anger intensifies from annoyance and disappointment to rage and destructive behavior.

Anger has both practical and spiritual consequences. Its great spiritual danger occurs when anger is "a purely selfish matter and the expression of a merely peevish vexation at unexpected and unwelcome misfortune or frustration" as when the Vols fumble at the Alabama five-yard line. It thus interferes with the living of the righteous, Christ-like life God intends for us.

Our own anger, therefore, can incur God's wrath; making God angry can never be anything but a perfectly horrendous idea.

Let me be an example to other kids who feel like they've got the weight of the world of their shoulders. It's hard, but there is a better way.
--Kevin Burnett

Anger becomes a problem when it escalates into rage and interferes with the righteous life God intends for us.

TENNESSEE

DAY 44

LEGAL THIEVERY

Read Exodus 22:1-15.

"A thief must certainly make restitution" (v. 2b).

Against Alabama in 1970, the Tennessee defense acted as though it had never heard an admonition against stealing. The Vols shamelessly picked off an incredible eight Tide passes.

At 28, Bill Battle was the youngest head football coach in the country when he took over the Vols following Doug Dickey's departure to lead the Gators. Battle won ten games and buried Air Force in the Sugar Bowl his rookie season of 1970. One of the highlights of the season was the meeting between Battle and his former coach, Bear Bryant. The Tide was 3-2, Tennessee 3-1 with a loss to Auburn when they collided in Knoxville on Oct. 17.

The thievery started early. On Alabama's second series of the game, Vol defensive back Tim Priest intercepted a deflected pass and returned it to the Tide 16. Priest, the team captain, would tie the school record with three interceptions in the game. He would also earn All-SEC honors in 1970 and would set the Vols' career interception record with 18 (which still stands).

UT took advantage of Priest's theft to take a 7-0 lead. Sophomore linebacker Jamie Rotella and two-time All-American linebacker Jackie Walker each had interceptions in the first half.

"Alabama didn't punt the entire last half. They didn't have to [because] Tennessee was picking the ball out of the air before they had the chance." Defensive back Conrad Graham, a 1972

VOLUNTEERS

All-American, grabbed the first Alabama pass of the last half. Two series later, Priest got his second interception. On the next Bama possession, defensive back Bobby Majors got one. On Bama's next play, Walker returned his second theft 22 yards for a touchdown. Priest later got his third interception, tying Albert Dorsey and Bill Young for the school record in a game.

Tennessee won 24-0. The eight interceptions against Alabama and the 36 interceptions that season remain the school records.

Buckle up your seat belt. Wear a bicycle or motorcycle helmet. Use your pooper scooper to clean up after your dog. Don't walk on the grass. Picky ordinances, picky laws – in all their great abundance, they're an inescapable part of our modern lives.

When Moses came stumbling down Mt. Sinai after spending time as God's secretary, he brought with him a whole mess of laws and regulations, many of which undoubtedly seem picky to us today. What some of them provide, though, are practical examples of what for God is the basic principle underlying the theft of personal property: what is wrong must be made right.

While most of us today probably won't have to worry too much about oxen, sheep, and donkeys, making what is wrong right remains a way of life for Christians. To get right with other people requires anything from restitution to apologies. To get right with God requires Jesus Christ.

All I could see was the red flag in the corner.
-- Jackie Walker on his interception return for a touchdown vs. Alabama

To make right the wrong of stealing
requires restitution; to make right
our relationship with God requires Jesus Christ.

DAY 45

WHO CARES?

Read Psalm 90.

"Teach us to number our days aright, that we may gain a heart of wisdom" (v. 12).

Laurie Milligan has a lesson for us: Don't take for granted anything precious in our lives.

On Sunday, Feb. 22, 1998, fans of the Lady Vols caught a glimpse of what might have been, of how the undefeated 1997-98 national champions – perhaps Tennessee's greatest team ever – could have been even better.

That day was Senior Day, and UT honored Milligan, its lone senior. She started and played for eleven minutes, contributing four points, three assists, and three steals in a 90-58 romp past LSU. One reporter said these rather pedestrian stats amounted to a "stunning performance." Therein lies the story.

Milligan started for UT as a junior and was averaging 8.3 points and 4.5 assists until she injured a knee against Alabama on Jan. 26, 1997. She underwent surgery and rehab, but this was not to be one of those feel-good comeback stories. The team's orthopedist discovered Milligan had a degenerative condition in the knee. He had only one recommendation for her: give up basketball.

Milligan played only once more that season. Coach Pat Summitt let her inbounds the ball in the final seconds of the win over Old Dominion that won the national championship. In her senior season, until Senior Night, she played in only one game, against

VOLUNTEERS

Portland in her home state. After all, she couldn't even practice and didn't dress out for games.

Milligan's mother drove all the way from Oregon for Senior Night and saw her daughter steal the ball, dribble it behind her back, and hit Semeka Randall with a strike for a layup. She and the crowd witnessed a flash of brilliance, a glimpse of that which might have been but was lost forever.

Our daily lives usually settle into a routine; most of us don't thrive in a state of ongoing chaos. The danger of such familiarity, however, is that we come to take for granted that which is precious in our lives: our family members, our health, our friends, the security of our jobs. We may even become careless about them to the point of indifference.

But as Laurie Milligan's experience illustrates, we can assume nothing about the permanence of anything in our lives. This includes our salvation, which all too many people take for granted. They assume that just because they know who Jesus is, because they live what the world considers to be a "good" life, and because they attend church now and then, that they are saved.

But salvation comes through a commitment to Jesus, a surrendering of our lives to his control, and a love for him that overwhelms us. Taking Jesus and our salvation for granted is a sure sign that such commitment, surrender, and love are lacking.

I always took for granted that I could play. Now I know what a gift it is.
-- Rebecca Lobo, after a knee injury

**The apathy involved in taking Jesus for granted
negates the commitment to him
that is necessary for our salvation.**

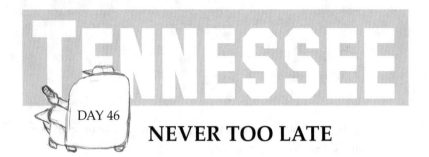

NEVER TOO LATE

Read Genesis 21:1-7.

"And [Sarah] added, 'Who would have said to Abraham that Sarah would nurse children? Yet I have borne him a son in his old age'" (v. 7).

It's something that everyone always asks you." Mike Stowell learned that even though it took twelve years, it was never too late to answer that question the way he wanted to.

Stowell was a four-year letterman (1989-1992) who played both offensive guard and tackle during his career. He was first-team All-SEC in 1992 and was part of two SEC championship teams while he wore the orange and white. In 2007, he was named the Vol Radio Network's sideline reporter for football broadcasts.

After he left the university, Stowell was repeatedly asked one question that always made him uncomfortable. When he told folks he played football for the Vols, they would inevitably ask him, "When did you graduate?" The answer for years was "I didn't." "You kind of hem and haw around and you can't really tell them with a straight face," Stowell said.

Eventually, Stowell's love for his daughter spurred him to action. He knew she would one day ask him the same question everybody else did, and he wanted to both set an example she could follow and give her an answer she could be proud of. After all, he needed only some foreign language requirements to complete his degree. He had a big problem, though; he lived in Idaho. That little matter of some big geography was resolved when the university let him meet those requirements at Idaho State University.

Thus, on Dec. 10, 2004, twelve years after he played his last game for Tennessee, Mike Stowell proudly graduated. From now on when someone asks him, he "can look them in the eye and say, 'It took me a while but I finally graduated.'"

Getting that college degree. Running a marathon. Getting married. Starting a new career. Though we may make all kinds of excuses, it's often never too late for life-changing decisions and milestones.

This is especially true in our faith life, which is based on God's promises. Abraham was 100 and Sarah was 90 when their first child was born. They were old folks even by the Bible's standards at the dawn of history. But God had promised them a child and just as God always does, he kept his promise no matter how unlikely it seemed.

God has made us all a promise of new life and hope through Jesus Christ. At any time in our lives – today even -- we can regret the things we have done wrong and the way we have lived, ask God in Jesus' name to forgive us for them, and discover a new way of living – forever.

It's never too late to change. God promised.

It's never too late to achieve success in sports.
> *-- Brooke de Lench, writer and lecturer on children and sports*

**It's never too late to change a life
by turning it over to Jesus.**

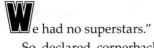

DAY 47

STAR POWER

Read Luke 10:1-3, 17-20.

"The Lord appointed seventy-two others and sent them two by two ahead of him to every town and place where he was about to go" (v. 1).

We had no superstars."

So declared cornerback Steve Johnson about his own team. Tight ends coach Mark Bradley was even more blunt. "I've been here nine years, and this is the fourth-most talented team we've had." So this was a mediocre team, right? No, it wasn't. It was, in fact, the 1998 national champions.

In the 1990s, the Tennessee football program produced some of the finest players in college and professional football history. The list starts with Heisman-Trophy runners-up Heath Shuler and Peyton Manning. But it also includes a number of offensive linemen like Charles McRae and Bubba Miller, running backs such as Jamal Lewis and Jay Graham, receivers like Carl Pickens, defensive linemen such as Leonard Little and Chuck Smith, and defensive backs like Dale Carter and Terry Fair.

None of those stars were around, however, on the night of Jan. 4, 1999, when the Vols met Florida State in the Fiesta Bowl for the national championship. The so-called experts must have taken a look at the Tennessee roster because they established the Vols as four-point underdogs to FSU and its stars.

How did this team so lacking in star power even make it to the

VOLUNTEERS

Fiesta Bowl? As Bradley went on to say, "It's the best team" he had seen at Tennessee. The no-name bunch came together as no other UT team had since 1951 and as no Vol team has done since. "Not one of them cares who gets the credit," said strength coach John Stucky. "That's what's so special."

They were no-names no longer after they whipped FSU 23-16 for the national title.

Football teams are like other organizations in that they may have a star but the star would be nothing without the supporting cast. It's the same in a private company, in a government bureaucracy, in a military unit, and just about any other team of people with a common goal.

That includes the team known as a church. It may have its "star" in the preacher, who is – like the quarterback or the company CEO – the most visible representative of the team. Preachers are, after all, God's paid, trained professionals.

But when Jesus assembled a team of seventy-two folks, he didn't have anybody on the payroll or any seminary graduates. All he had were no-names who loved him. And nothing has changed. God's church still depends on those whose only pay is the satisfaction of serving and whose only qualification is their love for God. God's church needs you.

We lost all the superstars last year to the NFL.
— Cornerback Steve Johnson on the 1998 squad

**Yes, the church needs its professional clergy,
but it also needs those who serve as volunteers
because they love God; the church needs you.**

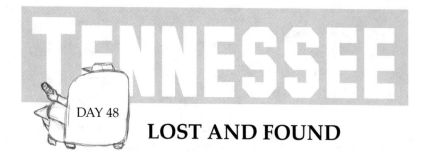

DAY 48

LOST AND FOUND

Read Luke 15:11-32.

"This brother of yours was dead and is alive again; he was lost and is found" (v. 32.

In search of some late-night munchies, two Volunteer basketball players lost a train.

Emmett Lowery coached the UT men's basketball team from 1948-59. With 168 wins, he retired as the winningest coach in school history. Lowery did not like to fly, so in the winter of 1953 when the Vols had a game against Florida in Gainesville, his team took the train.

The train had a one-hour layover in Atlanta, and that's when a couple of players got adventuresome. Ed Wiener and Carl Widseth had heard about a nearby all-night bakery. They were bona fide stars. As a senior in 1955, Wiener would be All-SEC and All-America. (See Devotion No. 61.) Widseth (1952-56) remains one of the greatest UT basketball players ever, named to the 20-man Team of the Century in 1990. A veteran sportswriter said in 2008 that Widseth "was the best back-to-the-basket player Tennessee has ever had to this day."

The duo figured they could get to that bakery and back to the train in plenty of time. "It was near midnight, so we pooled our money, got a cab and made a quick trip," Wiener said. The cabbie took them right to the bakery where they loaded up on cakes and cookies, climbed back into the cab, and soon pulled up into the train yard. And the train was nowhere in sight. It obviously had pulled out for Florida and left them behind. The two stood for a time, bewildered.

A brakeman came along and asked them what they were doing hanging around. When they explained, he laughed. Some cars had been unhitched and hooked to another train. "I think he pointed, but we were already moving on," Wiener said.

From car keys to friendships, fortunes to reading glasses, loss is a feature of the unfolding panorama of our lives. We win some, we lose some; that's life.

Loss may range from the devastatingly tragic to the momentarily annoying (such as a train in Atlanta). No loss, however, is as permanently catastrophic as the loss of our very souls. While "being lost" is one of Christianity's many complex symbols, the concept is simple: The lost are those who have chosen to separate themselves from God, to live without an awareness of God in an unrepentant lifestyle contrary to his commandments and tenets. Being lost is a state of mind as much as a way of life.

It's a one-sided decision, though, since God never leaves the lost; they leave him. No one is a born loser, and neither does anyone have to remain lost. All it takes is a turning back to God; all it takes is a falling into the open arms of Jesus Christ, the good shepherd.

Maybe we had lost our appetite.
-- Ed Wiener on the tasteless pastries after the lost train scare

**From God's point of view, we are all either lost
or found; interestingly, we – not God –
determine into which group we land.**

A ROARING SUCCESS

Read Galatians 5:16-26.

*"So I say, live by the Spirit. . . . The sinful nature desires
what is contrary to the Spirit. . . . The acts of the sinful
nature are obvious: . . . I warn you, as I did before, that
those who live like this will not inherit the kingdom of
God" (vv. 16, 17, 19, 21).*

Nowadays, the Vols' football season isn't deemed successful
because they beat Vanderbilt. Once, however, that was the case.

When Professor Nathan Dougherty, chairman of the athletic
council and captain of the 1909 football team, hired Capt. Bob
Neyland as head football coach prior to the 1926 season, he gave
Neyland only one directive: "Even the score with Vanderbilt. Do
something about the terrible series standings."

At the time, UT's record against the Commodores was 2-18-1.
The Vols had lost five straight in the series, most recently by scores
of 34-7 and 51-7. Neyland wasn't successful overnight against
Vanderbilt; he lost 20-3 in 1926 and gained what was then a moral
victory with a 7-7 tie in 1927. But then came 1928.

The Vols were 7-0 when they boarded the train for Nashville
and the Nov. 17 game. "Vol hysteria was gripping the eastern half
of the state" as several trainloads of Tennessee fans made the trip.
The crowd of 25,000 set a record in the state.

In the second quarter, Tennessee great Gene McEver (See Devotion No. 65.) returned a punt to the Vandy 24. After a holding

penalty against the Vols, he broke loose to the five. On fourth down from the 12, captain Roy Witt hit end Paul Hug, who fell across the goal line as he was tackled. The Vol defense intercepted five passes, and those six points stood up.

That game marked a permanent turnaround in the series. Neyland was 16-3-2 against Vandy as a head coach. He was, in a word, successful.

Are you a successful person? Your answer, of course, depends upon how you define success. Is the measure of your success based on the number of digits in your bank balance, the square footage of your house, that title on your office door, the size of your boat?

Certainly the world determines success by wealth, fame, prestige, awards, and possessions. Our culture screams that life is all about gratifying your own needs and wants. If it feels good, do it. It's basically the Beach Boys' philosophy of life.

But all success of this type has one glaring shortcoming: You can't take it with you. Eventually, Daddy takes the T-bird away. Like life itself, all these things are fleeting.

A more lasting way to approach success is through the spiritual rather than the physical. The goal becomes not money or backslaps by sycophants but eternal life spent with God. Success of that kind is forever.

Success demands singleness of purpose.

-- Vince Lombardi

**Success isn't permanent, and failure isn't fatal --
unless you're talking about
your relationship with God.**

FOOLPROOF

Read 1 Corinthians 1:18-31.

"For the message of the cross is foolishness to those who are perishing, but to us who are being saved it is the power of God" (v. 18).

In the fall of 1894, the university's athletic association made a decision so outlandish – and in hindsight so foolish – that to repeat it today would almost surely result in a run to local stores for some tar and feathers.

University of Tennessee football didn't exactly come charging out of the gate. The records of the first three seasons (1891-93) were 0-1, 2-5, and 2-4. The 1893 season was especially disappointing. The first four games were blowouts including the most lopsided loss in UT gridiron history. In the space of a four-day road trip, the Orange and White lost three times by an aggregate score of 194-0. After three seasons and fourteen games, Tennessee had yet to defeat a major foe.

That's when the athletic association made its dreadful decision, abolishing football to concentrate its energy and resources on baseball, which was the school's leading sport at the time. For instance, 2,500 fans made the road trip in 1892 to Maryville to watch a 16-10 UT win.

Who knows how subsequent history might have been different had not a transfer from Wake Forest decided to fight for a UT football team? William B. Stokely – of the Stokely-Van Camp

VOLUNTEERS

Company family – headed a group of students who lobbied for football's return. He even organized an informal team and scheduled three games, all of them victories. The athletic board relented and Tennessee fielded a football team in 1896.

Only during three wars (Spanish-American, WW's I and II) has Tennessee failed to field a team since that 1894-95 debacle.

Our culture proclaims that right now is all there is; hey, let's live for today with no worries about cause and effect. Many of us buy into that philosophy. Congress recklessly spends money the nation doesn't have. Like a mini-version of our legislators, we load up our credit cards far beyond our abilities to sustain. We treat our bodies as though we will never suffer any repercussions from drugs and alcohol or even from a lousy diet and no exercise.

So to live with an eye not only on tomorrow but on eternity is foolishness to the world. To regard our actions as having eternal consequences – what's up with that? To believe that we are responsible for where we spend life after death – to believe in an afterlife at all -- how foolish is that?

It's as foolish as almighty God himself, he who died on the cross to loose his saving power on a lost world overly prideful of its own foolish wisdom.

It is foolish to expect a young man to follow your advice and to ignore your example.
> *-- Basketball Coach Don Meyer*

**Through Jesus, God has turned our notions
of wisdom and foolishness
inside out and upside down.**

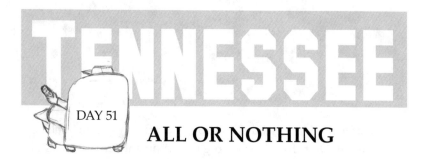

DAY 51

ALL OR NOTHING

Read Deuteronomy 6:4-9.

"Love the Lord your God with all your heart and with all your soul and with all your strength" (v. 5).

What in the world could make an Italian kid from New Orleans who had trouble understanding East Tennessee English decide to play football for UT, especially when his father had reservations? Love could.

In 1947, Hank Lauricella was called to the office of Holy Cross High School for a phone call. Gen. Bob Neyland was on the phone, and he invited Lauricella to Knoxville. Ole Miss was also recruiting him, so he scheduled a one-week recruiting trip with three days in both Knoxville and Oxford. Fortunately for Tennessee gridiron history, the trip to Knoxville came first.

Lauricella's first impression of Knoxville was how unusual the folks from East Tennessee talked. He had difficulty understanding them, but soon was able to catch most of what he heard. The coaches let him check out a uniform and run some plays. Lauricella promptly fell in love with everything about the place. "I really enjoyed myself," he recalled, "and decided not to bother with Oxford." He called the Rebs and canceled.

His father began to have second thoughts after his son signed a scholarship. Wouldn't LSU or Tulane be a better choice since they were closer to home? "I tried to explain how I had fallen in love with the University of Tennessee," Lauricella said. "My father

VOLUNTEERS

said, 'Well, if you really love the place . . .', and I said I did."

Tailback Hank Lauricella led UT to a 28-4-1 record his three seasons, including the 1951 national championship and a 20-game win streak. As a senior in 1951, he was voted All-America and finished second in the Heisman Trophy balloting. In 1981, he was elected to the College Football Hall of Fame, another honor for playing very well for the school he dearly loved.

Too many sports fans cheer loudly when their team is winning championships, but they're the first to criticize or turn silent when losses and disappointments come. Unlike Hank Lauricella, who never lost his love for UT, they're fair-weather fans.

True Tennessee fans stick with the Volunteers no matter what, which is exactly the way God commands us to love him. Sure, this mandate is eons old, but the principle it established in our relationship with God has not changed. If anything, it has gained even more immediacy in our materialistic, secular culture that demands we love and worship anything and anybody but God.

Moreover, since God gave the original command, he has sent us Jesus. Thus, we today are even more indebted to God's grace and have even more reason to love God than did the Israelites to whom the original command was given.

God gave us everything; in return, we are to love him with everything we have and everything we are.

All these years later, I still love the University of Tennessee.
-- Hank Lauricella

With all we have and all we are –
that's the way we are to love God.

DAY 52

CONQUERING HEROES

Read John 16:19-33.

"In this world you will have trouble. But take heart! I have overcome the world" (v. 33b).

She bought a little red wagon, just one of the unique ways a UT athletic pioneer overcame the obstacles she faced.

Susan Thornton was UT's first great female shot putter. She came to Knoxville in 1976 quite literally because of the flip of a discus. She was undecided about college until at the state track meet her senior year, she had a discus with an orange spot on one side for UT and a red spot on the other for NC State. She flung it as far as she could, and it landed with the orange dot up.

As a pioneer in a sport in which not many women participated, Thornton had to overcome a number of obstacles. For instance, she had no one to teach her how to use the shot. She was waiting around for volleyball practice to begin when she discovered her high school had a shot put. "No one knew why we had [one], and no one knew how to use it, but we had one," she said. She taught herself by using two socks to outline a circle, throwing into a sand pit, and watching world champion Brian Oldfield on TV.

At UT, money for equipment for women was limited in those early days, so she was responsible for her own gear. The problem was her gear weighed about 400 pounds. Each day, she had to carry to practice jump ropes, shot puts, a discus, shoes, and medicine balls. She overcame that problem by buying a little

VOLUNTEERS

red wagon that she pulled all across campus. She ruined two suitcases carrying her gear through airports before she bought an old metal suitcase from a junk store and fashioned some foam forms around her equipment.

Whatever the obstacle, Susan Thornton overcame it. Like her, we each have a choice to make about how we live. We can merely survive or we can overcome.

We often hear inspiring stories of people who triumph by overcoming especially daunting obstacles. Those barriers may be physical or mental disabilities or great personal tragedies or injustice. When we hear of them, we may well respond with a little prayer of thanksgiving that life has been kinder to us.

But all people of faith, no matter how drastic the obstacles they face, must ultimately overcome the same opponent: the Satan-infested world. Some do have it tougher than others, but we all must fight daily to remain confident and optimistic.

To survive from day to day is to give up by surrendering our trust in God's involvement in our daily life. To overcome, however, is to stand up to the world and fight its temptations that would erode the armor of our faith in Jesus Christ.

Today is a day to overcome by remaining faithful. The very hosts of Heaven wait to hail the conquering hero.

Many people were looking for ways to discount what we were doing. I would draw comments such as, 'You'll never be cute doing that.'
-- Susan Thornton on obstacles she had to overcome as a pioneer athlete

**Life's difficulties provide us a chance
to experience the true joy of victory in Jesus.**

DAY 53

THE SNAKE PIT

Read Matthew 23:29-39.

*"You snakes! You brood of vipers! How will you escape
being condemned to hell?" (v. 33)*

Snakes and bats. That's what Tennessee coaches encountered
with All-American guard Bill Mayo.

Mayo was a four-year starter for the Vols from 1981-84. At the
time, he set a school record by starting in 46 games, missing only
one game his sophomore season with an injury. His senior season
he was both All-SEC and All-America as the primary blocker
opening holes through which Johnny Jones ran for 1,290 yards.

Mayo definitely marched to a slightly different beat. Vol line
coach Phillip Fulmer once made the mistake of letting Mayo
talk him into a caving expedition. Mayo said that Fulmer "did
pretty well for the first hour or two." The spelunkers encountered a few tight places, which were a problem for the former
offensive lineman. Nevertheless, he managed to crawl through
on his stomach. So Fulmer was doing even better than everyone
expected until he placed a hand on a wall to steady himself. "He
put his hand on a bat," Mayo said.

Mayo played his high-school ball in Dalton, Ga. His primary
recruiter was Bobby Jackson, who coached at Tennessee from
1977-82, serving as running backs coach and both linebacker
coach and defensive coordinator. Jackson did a good job and had
Mayo pretty well sewed up, but head coach John Majors figured

a personal visit would seal the deal for this outstanding lineman they wanted badly. Fulmer and he drove to Mayo's home; the visit went well until Mayo pulled out his pet: an eight-foot-long python. Majors said he tried to be polite, but "I didn't want much to do with that snake."

Who would want to be known as a snake-in-the-grass? Or to be so unlucky, you're snake bit? Don't roll snake eyes if you're foolish enough to gamble, and don't drink any snake oil for medicinal help.

Snakes and mankind have never exactly been bosom buddies. The Old Testament often uses snakes (and serpents) as metaphors for something or someone who is dangerous and wicked. Thus, Jesus had a great scriptural tradition undergirding his referring to religious leaders as snakes.

Jesus' point was that the religious folks were wicked and dangerous because they appeared faithful and righteous on the outside while their hearts were not committed to the truth of the scripture they supposedly taught. That is, they failed to see Jesus for the savior he was and were leading their people to do the same, thus condemning them all to hell.

The insult still has meaning today, and God still has an awful fate reserved for the wicked snakes who turn their back on Jesus.

I've been a lot of things, but never a snake-handler.
— Head Coach John Majors on his visit to Bill Mayo's home

Snakes are the "almost" Christians,
the ones for whom faithfulness is a show
that doesn't reach their hearts.

TENNESSEE

DAY 54

MYSTERIOUS WAYS

Read Romans 11:25-36.

"O the depth of the riches and wisdom and knowledge of God! How unsearchable are his judgments and how inscrutable his ways!" (v. 33 NRSV)

Sometimes there is simply no explanation for what happens in a football game; it's just a mystery. Like a wide-open player falling down short of the goal line for no apparent reason.

That's what happened to Alabama against Tennessee in 1996. It was probably the play that meant the difference in the game.

As the game wore on, Tennessee fans found little to cheer about. Perhaps their loudest yells came after a play that didn't seem very important at the time. In the second quarter, Peyton Manning fumbled as he was sacked. An Alabama defender gobbled up the loose ball at the six-yard line. He could have quite literally walked into the end zone -- but he didn't. Incredibly, he stumbled and fell at the three.

There the Vol defense made a stand behind Jonathan Brown, Billy Ratcliff, and Raymond Austin. Leonard Little deflected a fourth-down field-goal try. Alabama went on to lead 13-0 in the third quarter, and only in retrospect did the importance of the player's mysterious stumble become apparent.

With 4:26 to go in the third, Manning hit Joey Kent with a 54-yard bomb for a score. A Terry Fair interception set up a Jay Graham run. With 9:41 to play, the game was suddenly tied at 13.

VOLUNTEERS

Then with only 2:17 left Graham turned Neyland Stadium into complete bedlam when he exploded for a 79-yard touchdown run. Tennessee won 20-13, a score that never would have happened had not that Alabama defender mysteriously fallen down.

People of faith understand that the good Lord does indeed work in mysterious ways. This only serves to make God even more tantalizing because human nature loves a good mystery. We relish the challenge of uncovering what somebody else wants to hide. We are intrigued by a perplexing whodunit, a rousing round of Clue, or Perry Mason reruns.

Some mysteries are simply beyond our knowing, however. Events in our lives that are in actuality the mysterious ways of God remain so to us because we can't see the divine machinations. We can see only the results, appreciate that God was behind it all, and give him thanks and praise.

God has revealed much about himself, especially through Jesus, but still much remains unknowable. Why does he tolerate the existence of evil? What does he really look like? Why is he so fond of bugs? What was the inspiration for chocolate?

We know for sure, though, that God is love, and so we proceed with life, assured that one day all mysteries will be revealed.

Through sports, a coach can offer a boy a way to sneak up on the mystery of manhood.
— Writer Pat Conroy

God chooses to keep much about himself
shrouded in mystery, but one day
we will see and we will understand.

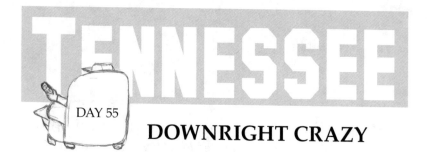

DOWNRIGHT CRAZY

Read Luke 13:31-35.

"Some Pharisees came to Jesus and said to him, 'Leave this place and go somewhere else. Herod wants to kill you.' He replied, 'Go tell that fox . . . I must keep going today and tomorrow and the next day'" (vv. 31-33).

Legendary UT linebacker Jack Reynolds is well known by what is perhaps the best nickname ever bestowed upon a linebacker: Hacksaw. His Tennessee teammates had another moniker for him: Crazy Jack.

Both nicknames are perhaps related to how Reynolds took out his frustration after a loss in 1969 to Ole Miss. Some dispute remains over what kind of vehicle it was, but there is no disputing that Reynolds sawed a vehicle in half with a hacksaw. The surgery required a dozen blades. "I had to do something to relieve my frustration," Crazy Jack explained.

"Reynolds was a funny duck," said P.W. Underwood, one of Hacksaw's coaches at UT. "Jack is a strange man," agreed Reynolds' mother-in-law, "but he's a good man."

Reynolds certainly had his own ways. Legendary UT center Bob Johnson (See Devotion No. 85.) recalled that during spring workouts in 1967 when Reynolds was a freshman, he would sprint all-out during warmups for agility drills. "It happened every day," Johnson said. "Jack would run like a wild man for 17 or 18 of those 50-yard warmups, then stop and throw up his lunch. He was a bizarre young man."

Reynolds' persona was somewhat carefully crafted, though. He relished the underdog role, wearing a tattered T-shirt that read, "Too old, too short, too slow and can't cover." He wanted to keep everyone off balance, wondering what he might do next.

What Crazy Jack really did was play football very well. He was All-SEC in both 1968 and '69 and All-America in 1969. He was a first-round pick of the Rams in 1970 and had a 14-year pro career that included two Super-Bowl wins.

As in Jack Reynolds' case, what some see as crazy often is shrewd instead. Like the time you went into business for yourself or when you went back to school. Maybe it was when you fixed up that old house. Or when you bought that new company's stock.

You know a good thing when you see it but are also shrewd enough to spot something that's downright crazy. Jesus was that way too. He knew that his entering Jerusalem was in complete defiance of all apparent reason and logic since a whole bunch of folks who wanted to kill him were waiting for him there.

Nevertheless, he went because he also knew that when the great drama had played out he would defeat not only his personal enemies but the most fearsome enemy of all: death itself.

It was, after all, a shrewd move that provided the way to your salvation.

Jack wasn't crazy; he was just different.

-- UT Coach Lon Herzbrun

It's so good it sounds crazy -- but it's not: through faith in Jesus, you can have eternal life with God.

DAY 56

JUST PERFECT

Read Matthew 5:43-48.

"Be perfect, therefore, as your heavenly Father is perfect"
(v. 48).

Tennessee's defense in 1939 was perfect, accomplishing a feat that almost surely will never again be duplicated in college football: They didn't allow a single point all season.

The ten Volunteer wins of 1939 were part of a stretch of 33 straight regular-season wins that began late in the 1937 season and continued through the 1941 opener. The only losses during that time were in bowl games. The win streak included an even more remarkable streak: 17 straight regular-season shutouts, an NCAA record that surely will never be broken.

The defensive perfection in 1939 was disputed by a Vanderbilt player. Against the Commodores, coach Bob Neyland followed his usual practice of resting his starters by pulling them with ten minutes to go in the first half. Vanderbilt promptly marched to the UT three against the reserves. A first-down smash into the line moved the ball to the one, leaving the Dores with three tries to move the ball 36 inches for a touchdown.

As everybody expected, Vanderbilt called on its powerful fullback, Roy Huggins. He "plowed into a small opening at right tackle, [and] quickly disappeared into a mass of humanity that included sophomore lineman Don Edmiston and several of his Volunteer pals." When the officials dispersed the pile of bodies, they placed the ball inches from the goal line.

Huggins always insisted he scored, but "in those days they didn't mark it as strictly by forward motion as they do now." Vanderbilt tried an end-around on third down and lost five yards. A fourth-down play went nowhere, and Vandy never threatened again. UT won 13-0 and went on to shut out Kentucky and Auburn to complete the perfect season of defense.

Nobody's perfect; we all make mistakes every day. We botch our personal relationships; at work we seek competence, not perfection. To insist upon personal or professional perfection in our lives is to establish an impossibly high standard that eventually destroys us physically, emotionally, and mentally.

Yet that is exactly the standard God sets for us. Our love is to be perfect, never ceasing, never failing, never qualified – just the way God loves us. And Jesus didn't limit his command to only preachers and goody-two-shoes types. All of his disciples are to be perfect as they navigate their way through the world's ambiguous definition and understanding of love.

But that's impossible! Well, not necessarily if to love perfectly is to serve God wholeheartedly and to follow Jesus with single-minded devotion. Anyhow, in his perfect love for us, God makes allowance for our imperfect love and the consequences of it in the perfection of Jesus.

I got in, but they pushed me back.
--Vanderbilt Fullback Roy Huggins on his run at the one

**In his perfect love for us, God provides a way
for us to escape the consequences
of our imperfect love for him: Jesus.**

DAY 57

STORY TIME

Read Luke 8:26-39.

"'Return home and tell how much God has done for you.'
So the man went away and told all over town how much
Jesus had done for him" (v. 39).

Track scholarship but a Hall-of-Fame basketball career. A room-mate's murder. Olympian who didn't get to play. Holly Warlick certainly has a story to tell.

Warlick's lifelong association with the Lady Vols and Pat Summitt began in 1976 when she arrived on campus with a scholarship for the 400-meter run. She walked onto the basketball team, though practically everyone did in those early days. "We weren't really into the scholarship scene," Summitt recalled. "I had just been given $3,000, and I gave it to three players who had already been there."

Up to that point, women's basketball at UT hadn't done much, but that all changed in a hurry. A three-time All-America, Warlick was the starting point guard for four seasons, was once dubbed the "best player in the South," and never played on a team that won fewer than 27 games. Her senior year, she became the first UT athlete of either gender to have a jersey retired.

Warlick was picked for the 1980 Olympic team that didn't get to go to Moscow because of the boycott. After her graduation in 1980, she played one season of pro ball with the Nebraska Wranglers. She broke a wrist and her nose, paychecks stopped coming, and her roommate was murdered. She still led the team to the title.

In 1985, Warlick returned home to UT as an assistant coach and stayed. The 2009-10 season marked her 25th year on Summitt's staff. She has been enshrined in five halls of fame, including the Women's Basketball Hall of Fame in which she entered in only the third class.

Yep, Holly Warlick has a story or two to tell.

So you didn't make the Olympic team, play pro basketball, or help establish a sports dynasty with your coaching abilities. You nevertheless have a story to tell; it's the story of your life and it's unique. No one else among the billions of people on this planet can tell the same story.

Part of that story is your encounter with Jesus. It's the most important chapter of all, but all too often believers in Jesus Christ don't tell it. Otherwise brave and daring Christian men and women who wouldn't think twice of skydiving or white-water rafting often quail when we are faced with the prospect of speaking about Jesus to someone else. It's the dreaded "W" word: witness. "I just don't know what to say," we sputter.

But witnessing is nothing but telling your story. No one can refute it; no one can claim it isn't true. You don't get into some great theological debate for which you're ill prepared. You just tell the beautiful, awesome story of Jesus and you.

I was just in the right place at the right time.
-- Holly Warlick on her career at UT

We all have a story to tell, but the most important part of all is the chapter where we met Jesus.

TRAGEDY

Read Job 1:1-2:10.

"In all this, Job did not sin by charging God with wrongdoing" (v. 1:22).

The 1965 Tennessee football season is often remembered for two of the most famous games ever, but that year also saw the greatest tragedy in the program's history.

The regular season ended when the Vols, headed to the Bluebonnet Bowl, upset Rose-Bowl bound UCLA 37-34. Quarterback Dewey Warren (See Devotion No. 41.) scored from the one on fourth down as time was running out.

The Alabama game ended bizarrely when, with the score tied at seven and Bama at the UT three, Tide quarterback Kenny Stabler threw the ball out of bounds to stop the clock with only six seconds left. Good execution -- bad idea. It was fourth down.

That strange tie, which left the Vols with a strange 2-0-2 mark, also left the players and the coaches in fine spirits as they anticipated the upcoming game against the Houston Cougars. Their exhilaration lasted only 48 hours, however.

At 6:53 a.m. on Monday, Oct. 18, in west Knoxville, a passenger train slammed into a car carrying three Volunteer assistant coaches to work. Killed on the scene were Bill Majors, the 26-year-old younger brother of John Majors and a standout tailback from 1958-60, and end coach Bob Jones, 30. Offensive line coach Charlie Rash, 28, died four days later.

VOLUNTEERS

"UT had never known tragedy of such magnitude." "You just don't play for coaches; you learn to love them and respect them," said team captain Hal Wantland. Houston graciously offered to cancel Saturday's game, but AD Bob Woodruff and coach Doug Dickey decided to go ahead. The players wore black crosses on their helmets. UT won 17-8, a victory that "had no real meaning in view of what had happened that week."

While we may receive them in varying degrees, suffering and tragedy are par for life's course. What we do with tragedy when it strikes us determines to a great extent how we live the rest of our lives. We can – in accordance with the bitter suggestion Job's wife offered -- "Curse God and die," or we can trust God and live. That is, we can plunge into endless despair or we can lean upon the power of a transcendent faith in an almighty God who offers us hope in our darkest hours.

We don't have to understand tragedy; we certainly don't have to like it or believe there's anything fair about it. What we must do in such times, however, is trust in God's all-powerful love for us and his promise that all things will work for good for those who love him. In choosing a life of ongoing trust in God in the face of our suffering, we prevent the greatest tragedy of all: that of a soul being cast into Hell.

The Tennessee players responded to the tragedy, and it made them closer and brought them together as a team.
-- Larry Majors, Bill Majors' younger brother

Tragedy can drive us into despair and death or into the life-sustaining arms of almighty God.

DAY 59

THE PRIZE

Read Philippians 3:10-16.

"I press on toward the goal to win the prize for which God has called me heavenward in Christ Jesus" (v. 14).

Volunteer tight end John Finlayson once received one of the most unusual awards in the school's football history: He was named All-America by *Successful Farming* magazine.

Finlayson started two games on the national championship team as a freshman and then was a three-year starter for the Vols from 1999-2001. He was used primarily as a blocker. His career-long 24-yard catch from Casey Clausen in 2000 led to the second touchdown of the record-setting 35-point first quarter against Arkansas (a 63-20 romp). Perhaps his biggest moment came in 2001 in the 34-32 win over Florida that sent the Vols to the SEC championship game. His recovery of the Gators' last-gasp onside kick clinched the win.

All four seasons in Knoxville, Finlayson was Academic All-SEC. And then there was that award from the magazine. Like his game, Finlayson wasn't a flashy individual. One writer noted that "the only giveaway that he's a football player is an occasional ice bag taped to his knee." Many of his classmates were never aware he was the Vols' starting tight end. "I kind of prefer it that way," he said. "When I leave the field, I like just being a regular student."

His subtlety was a product of his roots -- a farm near the Mississippi line. "Growing up we had hogs and cows and a few chickens on our farm," Finlayson said. "But I mostly worked at the farm supply store my parents owned." That agricultural background led to the award, which let him in for some ribbing from teammates. "I told him that *Field & Stream* is going to name him All-American next week," said fellow tight end Neil Johnson.

Even the most modest and self-effacing among us can't help but be pleased by prizes and honors. They symbolize the approval and appreciation of others, whether it's an All-American team, an Employee of the Month trophy, a plaque for sales achievement, or the sign declaring yours as the neighborhood's prettiest yard.

Such prizes and awards are often the culmination of the pursuit of personal achievement and accomplishment. They represent accolades and recognition from the world. Nothing is inherently wrong with any of that as long as we keep them in perspective.

That is, we must never let awards become such idols that we worship or lower our sight from the greatest prize of all and the only one truly worth winning. It's one that won't rust, collect dust, or leave us wondering why we worked so hard to win it in the first place. The ultimate prize is eternal life, and it's ours through Jesus Christ.

A gold medal is a wonderful thing, but if you're not enough without it, you'll never be enough with it.
-- *John Candy in* Cool Running

The greatest prize of all doesn't require competition to claim it; God has it ready to hand to you through Jesus Christ.

TENNESSEE

DAY 60

CHILD'S PLAY

Read John 1:6-18.

"Yet to all who received him, to those who believed in his name, he gave the right to become children of God" (v. 12).

Bob Suffridge had a rather interesting childhood.

Suffridge is one of the greatest linemen in both Tennessee and college football history, the best player on some of UT's greatest teams (11-0, 10-1, and 10-1). He is Tennessee's only three-time All-America (1938, '39, '40); he won the Knute Rockne Memorial Trophy in 1940 as the country's best lineman. When the Associated Press assembled a team of the half-century from 1900-50, Suffridge was at guard.

He started out life on a farm in East Tennessee chopping wood, plowing fields, milking cows, and slopping hogs. He said he grew up strong "on cornbread, beans and 'taters." He may have been involved in the making of some moonshine whiskey. When he was 11, his family moved to Knoxville, and he encountered indoor plumbing for the first time.

He once thought he had a job with the Works Progress Administration and spent a summer breaking rocks with a sledge-hammer. He never got paid, and when he asked the foreman about his money, he learned it had all gone to his father.

At 13, Suffridge ran away from home, but after three days, he hopped on a train and went back. "He was disappointed to discover his folks didn't even know he had been gone."

VOLUNTEERS

He was so good at football that the high-school coach played him even though he was in the eighth grade until the principal intervened. His father didn't want him to play, so Suffridge left again, taking up residence in the basement of a local doctor's office. The doctor bought him clothes and paid him for odd jobs.

As is the case with Bob Suffridge, childhood is often not the idyllic time we imagine it to be for the world's youngsters. That's because the parent-child relationship is founded on an imbalance of power, and the ones wielding the power frequently abuse it.

In his role as the creator of all life, God is in a sense the father of us all. Jesus, however, added a new layer of meaning to the traditional understanding of our relationship with God that truly renders us his children. Since only Christ is God's true son, only through Christ's mediation for us with God can the parent-child relationship be our own.

Our vision of a perfect childhood includes growth in a warm, safe, loving environment wherein the parent cherishes, protects, nurtures, and teaches the child. Love both restrains and guides the parent's power.

In other words, our vision of a perfect childhood matches God's vision for our relationship with him through Jesus.

It's really impossible for athletes to grow up. You're still a child, still playing a game.

-- Billie Jean King

**The physical act of birth places us in our parents'
family; the spiritual act of receiving Jesus Christ
as our Lord places us in God's family.**

DAY 61

WATER POWER

Read Acts 10:34-48.

"Can anyone keep these people from being baptized with water? They have received the Holy Spirit just as we have" (v. 47).

Socks were floating down the hall of an Atlanta hotel, proof positive that the Volunteer basketball team had way too much time on its hands.

When Tennessee played Georgia Tech on Feb. 16, 1953, the team stayed at the Peachtree Hotel. Ed Wiener was on the team. As a senior in 1955, he would be the team captain, All-SEC, and All-America. His roommate, J.D. Byington, who would be a three-year letterman, awakened him from a pregame nap. Wiener rolled over to see Byington standing on his bed and inspecting the overhead sprinkler system. In response to Byington's question that had awakened him, Wiener explained how the system worked. He tried to go back to sleep, but, said Wiener, "The next time I looked, J.D. was holding a match under the trigger [of the sprinkler system]. A moment later, we got wet."

And then some. Bells rang, fire trucks roared to the rescue, and the police showed up to contribute to the excitement and the panic. A desperate Byington tossed the matches into the toilet, but didn't flush them. When the first investigators opened the door to the room, a pair of socks floated out into the hall. "That's how bad it was," said Wiener. "At least two inches deep."

VOLUNTEERS

Officers found the incriminating matches and hauled Byington away. Coach Emmett Lowery hurried downtown, his main concern that Byington wouldn't be released in time for the game. He managed to talk the judge out of jail time and a hefty fine. Byington gratefully accepted the judge's lecture on social responsibility and agreed to pay for the damages.

The pair made it to the Tech gym before game time, and the Vols poured water all over Tech's evening by winning 82-79.

Children's wading pools and swimming pools in the backyard. Fishing, boating, skiing, and swimming at a lake. Sun, sand, and surf at the beach. If there's any water around, we'll probably be in it, on it, or near it. If there's not any at hand, we'll build a dam and create our own.

We love the wet stuff for its recreational uses, but water first and foremost is about its absolute necessity to support and maintain life. From its earliest days, the Christian church appropriated water as an image of life through the ritual of baptism. Since the time of the arrival of the Holy Spirit at Pentecost, baptism with water has been the symbol of entry into the Christian community. It is water that marks a person as belonging to Jesus. It is through water that a person proclaims that Jesus is his Lord.

There's something in the water, all right. There is life.

Swimmers are like tea bags; you don't know how strong they are until you put them in the water.

— Source unknown

There is life in the water:
physical life and spiritual life.

DAY 62

MUDSLINGING

Read Isaiah 1:15-20.

*"Though your sins are like scarlet, they shall be as white
as snow; though they are red as crimson, they shall be like
wool" (v. 18).*

Plain old-fashioned mud is one of the reasons the Volunteer
football team plays in such a magnificent structure today.

In the game's earliest days, Wait Field served as the home field.
It was not exactly a choice site; "rocks constantly work[ed] up from
the hard-packed surface to scrape elbows and knees. Spectators
watch[ed] games from wooden benches or seat[ed] themselves on
a high bank" on one side of the field.

In 1919, Col. W. S. Shields, president of City National Bank, paid
the balance owed on seven acres south of UT's hilltop campus for
use as an athletic field. Trustees voted to name the field in honor
of Shields and his wife, whose maiden name was Watkins.

Grandstands were erected in 1920, but in early 1921, the seats
overlooked "an unmarked, ungraded expanse of mounds and gul-
lies that turn[ed] into a quagmire in the rain." All classes were
cancelled for two days in March so students could shape the field
into something resembling playing conditions.

The first football game on the new field was played on Sept. 24,
1921, in a drizzling rain that illuminated a big problem: The field's
flat surface wouldn't drain. By 1925, the student newspaper was
deriding the field, declaring, "Fans are tired of seeing Tennessee's

VOLUNTEERS

wonderful football teams play in a sea of mud."

Before the 1926 season, Nathan Dougherty, chairman of the school's athletic council, had the playing surface sodded and molded into a turtle-back shape that eliminated the problem of the mud. The making of Shields-Watkins Field into the awesome Neyland Stadium of today had begun, in part because of mud.

Maybe you've never slopped any pigs. You may not be a fan of mud boggin'. Still, you've worked on your car, planted a garden, played touch football in the rain, or endured some military training. You've been dirty.

Dirt, grime, and mud aren't the only sources of stains, however. We can also get dirty spiritually by not living in accordance with God's commands, by doing what's wrong, or by not doing what's right. We all experience temporary shortcomings and failures; we all slip and fall into the mud.

Whether we stay there or not, though, is a function of our relationship with Jesus. For the followers of Jesus, sin is not a way of life; it's an abnormality, so we don't stay in the filth. We seek a spiritual bath by expressing regret and asking for God's pardon in Jesus' name. God responds by washing our soul white as snow with his forgiveness.

Making a field of Shields-Watkins will, if nothing more, reduce the athletic department's laundry bill.
– 1925 student newspaper criticizing the muddy football field

When your soul gets dirty, a powerful
and thorough cleansing agent is available
for the asking: God's forgiveness.

LIVE ACTION

Read James 2:14-26.

"Faith by itself, if it is not accompanied by action, is dead"
(v. 17).

Let's get a good one," coach Phillip Fulmer exhorted, but that was just talk -- until Peerless Price provided the action.

On Oct. 24, 1998, the third-ranked Vols hosted Alabama. UT was 6-0 for the first time since 1969 and seriously thinking about a national championship. The Big Orange was 4-0 in the SEC and was already in control of its own destiny in the conference. Thus, a loss to Alabama would have been catastrophic.

The Vols hurried down the field with the opening possession, covering 76 yards in seven plays. Quarterback Tee Martin got the score on a sneak from the one after he hit Cedrick Wilson for 18 yards. With 4:43 left in the second quarter, Martin rolled left for five yards to cap a 77-yard drive that propelled UT to a 14-3 lead.

But this was Alabama, remember. The Tide scored with 5:11 to go in the third and then converted the two-point conversion. The game was anybody's at 14-11, and the third largest crowd in Neyland Stadium history was officially nervous. The players, too, were well aware of the situation. "I knew momentum was kind of shifting their way," Price said.

That's when Fulmer gathered his kickoff team around and urged them to "get a good one." They didn't; instead, "they got a great one." Inserted just that day as a return man for the first time

VOLUNTEERS

since he suffered a broken ankle in 1997, Price gathered in the kickoff at the goal line and headed down the sideline. "Peerless blew down the Bama sideline like a blur," said linebacker Raynoch Thompson, who watched from across the field. Price wound up tying the school record with a 100-yard touchdown return. "They ran it back so fast, I didn't get a chance to sit down and get a drink of water," said Alabama's Shaun Alexander.

Price's action after Fulmer's talk effectively finished the Tide. On their way to the national championship, the Vols won 35-18, their fourth straight win over Alabama.

Talk is cheap. Consider your neighbor or coworker who talks without saying anything, who makes promises she doesn't keep, who brags about his own exploits, who can always tell you how to do something but never shows up for the work.

How often have you fidgeted through a meeting, impatient to get on with the work everybody is talking about doing? You know – just as Peerless Price and his teammates knew against Alabama -- that talk without action just doesn't cut it.

That principle applies in the life of a person of faith too. Merely declaring our faith isn't enough, however sincere we may be. It is putting our faith into action that shouts to the world of the depth of our commitment to Christ. Just as Jesus' ministry was a virtual whirlwind of activity, so are we to change the world by doing.

Jesus Christ is alive; so should our faith in Him be.

Don't talk too much or too soon.

-- Bear Bryant

Faith that does not reveal itself in action is dead.

TEARS TO TRIUMPH

Read Matthew 27:45-50, 55-61.

*"Many women were there, watching from a distance.
They had followed Jesus from Galilee to care for his
needs" (v. 55).*

Die-hard fans of the UT men's basketball program must have been in tears after the 1977-78 season. One season later, though, the tears were changed to shouts of triumphs after one of the most remarkable turnarounds in Vol sports history.

Three elements combined to send the program into a sudden tailspin in 1977: 1) Ernie Grunfeld was gone; 2) Bernard King was gone; 3) coach Ray Mears was gone, stepping down because of his health. Under an interim coach, UT skidded to 11-16, 6-12 in the SEC. Even the administration realized the program had fallen on hard times dizzyingly fast. They hired a "hot young coach" named Don DeVoe from Ohio State and warned him "it would be a while before we would be able to win." They said the school just didn't have the players on hand it took to win in the SEC.

DeVoe didn't see it that way, though. "I saw tremendous potential when I accepted the job," he said. "To me, there was no doom and gloom about the players returning."

DeVoe was right. His 1978-79 squad went 21-12, 12-6 in the conference, good for second place. Junior center Reggie Johnson led the team, averaging 21.1 points and 7.7 rebounds per game. Senior forward Terry Crosby scored 14.1 a game, and freshman

VOLUNTEERS

Gary Cater came out of nowhere to score 10.9 points a night.

What they did went beyond the record, though. They became the first UT team in history to beat Kentucky three times in a season, the last time in the finals of the newly reinstated SEC tournament. The team then forever notched its place in school lore by beating Eastern Kentucky for Tennessee's first win ever in the NCAA Tournament.

In one season, the Vols went from tears to triumph.

We all have times of defeat and loss in our lives, but nothing fills us with such an overwhelming sense of helplessness as the death of a loved one. There's absolutely nothing you can do about it. Like the women who stood at a distance and watched Jesus die on the darkest, bleakest day in history, you, too, can only stand helpless and weep as something precious and beautiful leaves your life.

For the believer in Jesus Christ and his loved ones, though, the Sunday of resurrection – the grandest, most triumphant day in history – follows the Friday of death. Faith in Jesus transforms loss into triumph, not only for the loved one but for those left behind. Amid your tears and your sense of loss, you celebrate the ultimate victory of your family member or friend. Amid death, you find life; amid sorrow, you find hope.

What a way to die! What a way to live!

The triumph cannot be had without the struggle.

– Wilma Rudolph

**Faith in Jesus Christ transforms death
from the ultimate defeat to the ultimate victory.**

DAY 65

GRAND ENTRANCE

Luke 2:1-20.

"She gave birth to her firstborn, a son. She wrapped him in cloths and placed him in a manger, because there was no room for them in the inn" (v. 7).

Eleven seconds. That's all it took for one of Tennessee's greatest football players to become a legend.

Gen. Robert Neyland called Gene McEver "the best player I ever saw." He was UT's first All-America and the first Volunteer to be inducted into the College Football Hall of Fame. His 21 touchdowns and 130 points in 1929 remain school records for a season.

A Tennessee high school was to play a Virginia squad that featured McEver as its star. The head coach asked Neyland for some help with the defense. Neyland later received a short note to the effect that the defense worked fine and McEver didn't do much from scrimmage. "Unfortunately," the coach wrote, "we had to punt five times. He returned all five for touchdowns."

After three wins in the fall of 1928, the Vols took on heavily favored Alabama. The opening kickoff "would go down as one of the most dramatic plays in Tennessee football history." McEver gathered in the ball" under a full head of steam at the UT 2." He headed up the middle, obviously faster than everybody else on the field. For most of the run, nobody was close to him. "Two guys hit me at the 40," McEver recalled, "and bounced off. After that, it was just me and the goalline."

McEver caught a touchdown pass from Bobby Dodd, and Farmer Johnson blocked an Alabama punt for a safety that was the margin in the 15-13 upset. For many, this was the beginning of Tennessee as a football powerhouse. On this day, just as Gene McEver did, the Vols made their grand entrance on the national stage.

A splashy grand entrance is certainly a crowd pleaser. Entertainment reporters breathlessly prowl the red carpet at awards shows to gush over the starlets who have carefully chosen a wardrobe designed for maximum effect and attention. The U.S. president strides into view while a band plays "Hail to the Chief." Nobody but nobody, however, tops the grand entrance the Volunteers make on game day at Neyland Stadium.

And then there's Jesus. Being God, he certainly could have make the grandest entrance of all, riding down from the heavens in a fiery chariot and coming as a full-grown warrior full of wrath, fury, and righteous indignation.

Instead, he entered this world relatively unnoticed, as a helpless baby tended by a teenaged peasant mother and watched over by some livestock. He will return, though, and next time he will make the grandest entrance of them all. He will come as the King of Kings to claim his kingdom. We had all better be ready.

I caught it and took off like a jackrabbit.
-- Gene McEver on his legendary kickoff return

**Jesus has made one less-than-grand entrance; the
next time he shows up will be entirely different.**

DAY 66

GOOD SPORTS

Read Titus 2:1-8.

"Show integrity, seriousness and soundness of speech that cannot be condemned, so that those who oppose you may be ashamed because they have nothing bad to say about us" (vv. 7b, 8).

On a Saturday afternoon in 1970, Tennessee's fans pulled off an unprecedented act of sportsmanship by paying their respects to a coach who had jilted them.

Quite a few folks were shocked when 31-year-old Doug Dickey was hired as UT's head football coach after the 1963 season. More than quite a few were shocked when he up and left for Florida before the Gator Bowl (against Florida) in 1969.

When Dickey arrived, the Vols had not won more than six games in a season in six years. He "conducted a football revival in Big Orange Country. The Volunteers were born again, transformed into winners as they had once been." After a 4-5-1 start in 1964, Dickey's Vols never failed to win fewer than eight games. UT won the SEC in 1967 and 1969. They beat Alabama three straight times. Dickey "was a resounding six-year success."

And then suddenly he left to return to his alma mater, the Florida Gators. He tried to keep his decision a secret since the two teams were to meet each other in the Gator Bowl on Dec. 27, but UPI broke the story. "Consorting with the Gators while preparing to play 'em was more than some Tennessee fans could swallow.

Dickey was finished before he officially resigned."

As the schedule would have it, Dickey returned to Knoxville in 1970. "It was not a picnic in the park. Revenge was taken." Tennessee massacred the Gators 34-7.

As Dickey trudged off the familiar turf of Shields-Watkins Field, thousands of classy UT fans gave him a standing ovation, thanking him for six great years. A surprised and teary-eyed Dickey tipped his cap at their sportsmanship.

One of life's paradoxes is that many who would never cheat on the tennis court or the racquetball court to gain an advantage think nothing of doing so in other areas of their life. In other words, the good sportsmanship they practice on the golf course or even on the Monopoly board doesn't carry over. They play with the truth, cut corners, abuse others verbally, run roughshod over the weaker, and generally cheat whenever they can to gain an advantage on the job or in their personal relationships.

But good sportsmanship is a way of living, not just of playing. Shouldn't you accept defeat without complaint (You don't have to like it.); win gracefully without gloating; treat your competition with fairness, courtesy, generosity, and respect? That's the way one team treats another in the name of sportsmanship. That's the way one person treats another in the name of Jesus.

One person practicing sportsmanship is better than a hundred teaching it.
-- Knute Rockne

Sportsmanship -- treating others with courtesy,
fairness, and respect -- is a way of living,
not just a way of playing.

DAY 67

PROMISES, PROMISES

Read 2 Corinthians 1:16-20.

*"No matter how many promises God has made, they are
'Yes' in Christ" (v. 20).*

Tennessee coach Pat Summitt kept one promise that required
she break another one.

Early in her career, Summitt promised that if she ever won
three national championships, she would retire. That day came on
March 31, 1991, when the Lady Vols beat Virginia 70-67. Summitt
had previously won titles in 1987 and 1989, but her coaching
career seemed safe as the 1990-91 season unwound and the Vols
went only 6-3 in the SEC. They lost to LSU in the SEC Tournament
finals and entered the Big Dance with a 25-5 record.

Wins over S.W. Missouri State, Western Kentucky, and Auburn
propelled the Vols to the Final Four in New Orleans. They defeated
the Stanford Cardinal, the defending national champs, 68-60 to
advance to the finals against what most pundits considered the
most talented team in the country.

The night belonged to Tennessee's junior point guard Dena
Head, who played what was called "the quintessential game
of [her] sterling career." As a senior in 1991-92, Head would be
All-America and the SEC Player of the Year. In 1997, she would be
the first player ever drafted into the WNBA.

Against Virginia, she tied the championship game record with
28 points. With seven seconds left, she hit a pair of free throws to

send the game into overtime. She then hit five charity shots in OT as UT outscored Virginia 10-7 for the 70-67 upset.

And Summitt's third national championship. She recalled her promise but broke it in favor of another one she had made. She had a great recruiting class on the way and said, "I promised those kids that I would be at Tennessee four years." As history records, she kept that promise.

The promises you make don't say much about you; the promises you keep tell everything.

The promise to your daughter to be there for her softball game. To your son to help him with his math homework. To your parents to come see them soon. To your spouse to remain faithful until death parts you. And remember what you promised God?

You may carelessly throw promises around, but you can never outpromise God, who is downright profligate with his promises. For instance, he has promised to love you always, to forgive you no matter what you do, and to prepare a place for you with him in Heaven.

And there's more good news in that God operates on this simple premise: Promises made are promises kept. You can rely absolutely on God's promises. The people to whom you make them should be able to rely just as surely on your promises.

In the everyday pressures of life, I have learned that God's promises are true.
                                        -- Major Leaguer Garret Anderson

**God keeps his promises just as those
who rely on you expect you to keep yours.**

DAY 68

SOUND OFF!

Read Revelation 4:1-10, 5:6-14.

"Then I looked and heard the voice of many angels, numbering thousands upon thousands, and ten thousand times ten thousand" (v. 11a).

Of course, the coaches and players are responsible for a football team winning a national championship. In Tennessee's 1998 run to the title, however, the fans proved crucial in one of the biggest games of the year.

When the sixth-ranked Vols hosted the second-ranked Florida Gators on Sept. 19 in the second game of the season, few pundits were speaking of a UT national championship other than as a distant hope that all fans have at season's beginning. That changed after Tennessee whipped the Gators 20-17 in an overtime classic.

An impartial observer could well remark that had the Gators played flawlessly, they would have whipped the Vols. After all, they handily outgained UT 396 yards to 235. They didn't play flawlessly, though; that's where the fans came in. They were so loud, so noisy, that they were a factor in the outcome.

In a game that was pivotal to both teams' hopes for a great season, the Gators committed five turnovers, and ultimately they couldn't overcome them. The turnovers and other UF mistakes were a direct result of the crowd noise; Florida quarterback Jesse Palmer admitted as much.

The noise "made it hard to audible," Palmer said. "Our center was having a hard time hearing the cadence." Florida was often late getting plays into the game, which left the offense little time for an audible, and the bedlam in Neyland Stadium only made the situation virtually impossible.

Senior Jeff Hall kicked a 41-yard field goal in OT; the Gators then missed a kick to tie. Needless to say, the crowd went wild.

Neyland Stadium erupts in a cacophony on game day. Loud music blares from the rattling speakers in the car next to you at the traffic light. The garbage men bang the cans around as though they receive bonuses for waking you up. A silence of any length in a conversation makes us uncomfortable; somebody please say something.

We live in a noisy world, which means activity, busyness, progress, and engagement with life. The problem with all that noise – however constructive it may be – is that it drowns out God's gentle voice. Thus, some quiet time each day is absolutely imperative if we are to grow our relationship with God. The intentional seeking of silence in which to hear God's voice constitutes surrender to the divine.

Though much about Heaven will be strange, we should be quite comfortable there. Revelation's lengthy description of God's home makes it very clear that it's a noisy place reverberating with the inspiring, exhilarating, and awesome sound of worship.

They're not going to beat us because their fans make a lot of noise.
-- Miami QB Vinny Testaverde before UT won 35-7

Heaven is a quite noisy place, echoing constantly with the wonderful sounds of worship.

FOUND WANTING

Read Psalm 73:23-28.

*"Whom have I in heaven but you? And earth has nothing
I desire besides you" (v. 25).*

Watching a Volunteer football game, a mother expressed her
heart's fondest desire: that her son score a touchdown. And then
Tennessee fumbled.

The Vols of 1956 were one of UT's greatest teams. Led by
tailback Johnny Majors, they went 10-1, won the SEC, and finished
with a No. 2 ranking. One of the leaders on that team was senior
right tackle and captain John Gordy. Though he didn't play football until his senior year of high school, Gordy won a scholarship to Tennessee, became a two-year starter, and was a Pro-Bowl
guard three times with the Detroit Lions.

On Nov. 24, the Vols took on Kentucky at home. They opened
the game with a 16-play drive that took the ball deep into Wildcat territory. John Gordy's mom was present at the game, watching with Majors' mother. She said that Gordy had never scored a
touchdown and that she'd give anything if he could. Mrs. Majors
astutely pointed out that tackles never score touchdowns.

With the ball at the Kentucky 7, the Vols did what they usually
did that season: they gave the ball to Majors off right tackle behind
Gordy. This time, though, Majors ran right smack into a Wildcat
defender. "I had the football in the wrong hand," Majors recalled,
and the Kentucky defender knocked the ball loose.

But the Vols caught a break. The ball "squirted out and hit Fangs right in the chest," Majors said. "That's what we called Gordy because his front teeth were missing and his eyeteeth looked like fangs." Gordy caught the ball and plodded his way into the end zone for a touchdown, dragging a couple of defenders with him.

His mom had her fondest wish.

What do you want out of life? A loving, caring family, a home of your own, the respect of those whom you admire? Our heart's desires can elevate us to greatness and goodness, but they can also plunge us into destruction, despair, and evil. Drugs, alcohol, control, sex, power, worldly success: Do these desires motivate you?

Desires are not inherently evil or bad for you; after all, God planted the capacity to desire in us. The key is determining which of your heart's desires are healthful and are worth pursuing and which are dangerous and are best avoided.

Not surprisingly, the answer to the dilemma lies with God. You consult the one whose own heart's desire is for what is unequivocally best for you, who is driven only by his unqualified love for you. You match what you want for yourself with what God wants for you. Your deepest heart's desire must be the establishment and maintenance of an intimate relationship with God.

An awesome attitude is best described as a "bad case of the wants."
-- Former Football Coach Erk Russell

**Whether our desires drive us to greatness
or to destruction is determined by whether
they are also God's desires for our lives.**

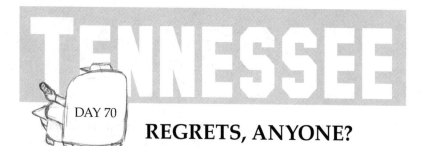

REGRETS, ANYONE?

Read 2 Corinthians 7:8-13.

"Godly sorrow brings repentance that leads to salvation and leaves no regret" (v. 10).

Tony Harris has never regretted playing basketball for the Vols even though in effect he had to be recruited twice.

Harris was a key ingredient of one of the greatest stretches in UT men's basketball history. From 1997-2001, the point guard led the Vols to four straight NCAA Tournament appearances and the SEC championship in 1999-2000. The UT men were 20-9, 21-9, 26-7, and 22-11 during Harris' four years in Knoxville. He was first-team All-SEC in 2000.

Harris was one of Coach Kevin O'Neill's prize recruits but never played for him. Five days after the 1996-97 season ended, O'Neill bolted for Northwestern. With O'Neill's abrupt departure, his prize recruits of Harris, Vincent Yarbrough, and Isiah Victor considered requesting releases from their scholarships. "I came close," Harris admitted. "I felt I wanted to go to Kansas."

On April 1, 1997, Jerry Green was named the new men's head coach. His most pressing problem was the virtual mutiny he had on his hands with the players already in Knoxville. He wisely sought advice from Pat Summitt. "I don't release anybody," she told him. Green called his team together and told them that if anybody wanted to leave they had to leave immediately or they would not be released. Two players left.

VOLUNTEERS

That didn't mean Harris would honor his scholarship, though, and Green set out to re-recruit him. He went to Harris' home in Memphis armed with a video of his 1996-97 Oregon Ducks, who ran, ran, and ran some more. "I was real impressed with that videotape," Harris said. "When I saw his style of play, I thought, 'This guy can come in and do some things.'" He reaffirmed his commitment to the Vols and never regretted it.

In their hit "The Class of '57," the Statler Brothers served up some pure country truth when they sang, "Things get complicated when you get past 18." That complication includes regrets; you have them; so does everyone else: situations and relationships that upon reflection we wish we had handled differently.

Feeling troubled or remorseful over something you've done or left undone is not necessarily a bad thing. That's because God uses regrets to spur us to repentance, which is the decision to change our ways. Repentance in turn is essential to salvation through Jesus Christ. You regret your un-Christlike actions, repent by promising God to mend your ways, and then seek and receive forgiveness for them.

The cold, hard truth is that you will have more regrets in your life. You can know absolutely, however, that you will never ever regret making Jesus the reason for that life.

I have no regrets about any decisions I made regarding my basketball career.
-- Tony Harris

**Regrets are part of living,
but you'll never regret living for Jesus.**

IMPORTANT STUFF

Read Matthew 6:25-34.

"Seek first his kingdom and his righteousness, and all these things will be given to you as well" (v. 33).

Haskel Stanback had his priorities in order: pretty girls and warm weather. So he wound up playing football for Tennessee.

In 1972 and '73, Stanback carried the load at tailback for the Vols, leading them to ten wins including a Bluebonnet-Bowl win over LSU in 1972 and the Gator Bowl in 1973. He was the Tennessee MVP of the Gator Bowl and finished his Volunteer career with 1,730 yards, ranking him 18th all time today.

From Kannapolis, N.C., Stanback was heavily recruited, but he seriously considered only three schools: Georgia Tech, Ohio State, and Tennessee. Those schools, however, had to meet his top two priorities: that the weather be warm and the girls be pretty.

One visit to Georgia Tech and its virtually all-male student population eliminated the Yellow Jackets. Stanback told athletic director and legendary Tech coach Bobby Dodd that he hoped to meet his wife in college, "but the pickings looked awful slim at Georgia Tech." Dodd suggested that Stanback "go out and find us some girls, and we'll recruit them for Georgia Tech." Bummer.

The Buckeyes were the early frontrunner, but a trip to Columbus, Ohio, also eliminated them from consideration. "It was the first time I'd been on a plane and when I flew out of Charlotte it was 60 degrees," Stanback recalled. It was snowing, though, when he landed in Columbus. "I don't mind playing football in the snow, but I don't want to have to walk around in snow as a regular thing," Stanback said. Ohio State was out.

The decision after Stanback's two trips was easy: It was Tennessee with its its temperate weather and its abundance of pretty girls. Incidentally, while he was in Knoxville, Stanback did indeed meet the woman who would become his wife.

Beautiful women and sunshine may not be the most important things in your life, but you do have priorities. What is it that you would surrender only with your dying breath? Every dime you have? Your family? Your Tennessee season tickets?

What about God? Would you denounce your faith in Jesus Christ rather than lose your children? Or everything you own?

God doesn't force us to make such unspeakable choices; nevertheless, followers of Jesus Christ often become confused about their priorities because so much in our lives clamors for attention and time. It all seems so worthwhile.

But Jesus' instructions are unequivocal: Seek God first. Turn to him first for help, fill your thoughts with what he wants for you and your life, use God's character as revealed in Jesus as the pattern for everything you do, and serve and obey him in all matters, at all moments.

God – and God alone – is No. 1.

If you've ever heard me at a press conference, the first thing I do is give honor to God because he's first in my life.
-- College Basketball Coach Gary Waters

God should always be number one in our lives.

DAY 72

FAITHFUL LIVES

Read Hebrews 11:1-12.

"Faith is the substance of things hoped for, the evidence of things not seen" (v. 1 NKJV).

Tennessee cornerback Jason Allen demonstrated he was a man of quite impressive faith when he said, "I never thought we'd lose this game." "This game" was one of the most exciting, heartstopping games in Volunteer history, the five-overtime 51-43 win over Alabama in 2003.

The five-hour marathon was rather pedestrian for most of the day until "all of a sudden a thriller broke out." Surely Allen had some doubts when Alabama led 20-13 in regulation and the Vols sat at their own 14 with only 1:52 left. But Casey Clausen marched the team to a touchdown on a 1-yard toss to Troy Fleming. When Alabama missed a field goal, it was on to overtime.

Where the teams couldn't stop scoring in spite of themselves. Derrick Tinsley's 6-yard catch got the point parade started, but Alabama answered. 27-27. Second overtime.

The Tide scored, and surely the faith of the Vol faithful must have wavered when UT faced fourth and 19 at the 34. But Clausen came through; he found C.J. Fayton down at the 5 and then hit James Banks for the score. 34-34. Third overtime.

On the first snap, Clausen hit Banks again for another TD, but the Vols failed on the two-point try. Alabama had an answer, but Jabari Green nabbed an interception on the conversion that would

VOLUNTEERS

have won the game for Alabama. 40-40. Fourth overtime.
A field goal each. 43-43. Fifth overtime.

Corey Larkins went for 14 and 7 yards and Clausen got the last four. He found Banks yet again for the conversion. On fourth down from the 17, Alabama went for the touchdown. Making only his second career start, Allen, the one of the great faith, batted a Tide pass away in the end zone to finally end the game.

Your faith forms the heart and soul of what you are. Faith in people, things, ideologies, and concepts to a large extent determines how you spend your life. You believe in the Volunteers, in your family, in the basic goodness of Americans, in freedom and liberty, and in abiding by the law. These beliefs mold you and make you the person you are.

This is all great stuff, of course, that makes for decent human beings and productive lives. None of it, however, is as important as what you believe about Jesus. To have faith in Jesus is to believe his message of hope and salvation as recorded in the Bible. True faith in Jesus, however, has an additional component; it must also include a personal commitment to him. In other words, you don't just believe in Jesus; you live for him.

Faith in Jesus does more than shape your life; it determines your eternity.

To me, religion – faith – is the only real thing in life.
                                                    -- Bobby Bowden

**Your belief system is the foundation
upon which you build a life; faith in Jesus
is the foundation for your eternal life.**

MEMORY LOSS

Read 1 Corinthians 11:17-29.

"[D]o this in remembrance of me" (v. 24).

As long as Tennessee plays the game, Vol football faithful will remember the magnificent 1956 battle with Georgia Tech." So wrote sportswriter Ben Byrd, who called it "the greatest football game I ever saw." The game was so great that a later poll selected it as the second-greatest college game ever played (behind only the 1935 game between Ohio State and Notre Dame).

On Nov. 10, 1956, at Grant Field, No. 2 Georgia Tech hosted No. 3 Tennessee. Legendary Tech coach Bobby Dodd had already said this was the finest team he had ever had.

What the game lacked in offense it more than made up for in constant, relentless tension. "Every play bore the weight of life and death." The game also displayed the remarkable courage and grit of a Tennessee team that refused to surrender. For the Vols, the defense "gave inches where yards were needed, first downs where touchdowns were necessary."

Tech's best shot at scoring came in the second quarter. They had a second down at the Volunteer 21, but Jim Smelcher fell on a fumble to end what would be the Yellow Jackets' only real chance at a touchdown.

As so often happens in a gruesome defensive struggle, the outcome of the game was decided suddenly. In the third quarter, Tennessee had a first down at the Tech 46 when All-American end Buddy Cruze showed why he was so honored. He shed a defensive back, Johnny Majors' pass was true, and Cruze was off and running. He was stopped at the one, but fullback Tommy Bronson -- for whom with teammate Bill Johnson the Tennessee football locker room is named -- scored on the next play.

Late in the game, interceptions by Bronson and Bubba Howe thwarted Tech drives. The Vols had a win to remember forever.

Memory makes us who we are. Whether our memories are dreams or nightmares, they shape us and to a large extent determine our actions and reactions. Alzheimer's is so terrifying because it steals our memory from us and in the process we lose ourselves. We disappear.

The greatest tragedy of our lives is that God remembers. In response to that memory, he condemns us for our sin. On the other hand, the greatest joy of our lives is that God remembers. In response to that memory, he came as Jesus to wash even the memory of our sins away.

Through memory, we encounter revival. At the Last Supper, Jesus instructed his disciples and us to remember. In sharing this unique meal with fellow believers and remembering Jesus and his actions, we meet Christ again not just as a memory but as an actual living presence. To remember is to keep our faith alive.

I don't want them to forget Babe Ruth. I just want them to remember Hank Aaron.

-- Hank Aaron

**We remember Jesus, and God
will not remember our sins.**

BRAGGING RIGHTS

Read Job 38.

"Have you ever given orders to the morning, or shown the dawn its place?" (v. 12)

Skeptical UT golf coaches listened to the high-school senior they were recruiting and figured she was bragging. She wasn't.

Despite battling injury as an upperclassman, Nicole Smith completed a stellar career at UT with the 2008-09 season. She was an Academic All-American Scholar three times, honorable mention All-SEC in 2006-07, and second-team All-SEC as both a freshman and a sophomore. She set the record for the lowest score ever by a freshman at the NCAA East Regionals.

Throughout her career in high school in California and in Knoxville, she was known for her prodigious tee shots. "I love teeing off first," she once said. "I hit it and walk off." But Smith didn't just hit the ball. As one reporter said, "She wallops it about 280 to 285 yards on average. She cranks out the kinds of tee shots that turn heads like bar stools."

During an unofficial recruiting visit, Smith told the Tennessee coaches what to expect from her. She matter-of-factly said that she could really hit the ball hard. Real hard. "I don't think they believed me," Smith said. UT coach Judy Pavon was among the skeptics, figuring she just had a bragging high-schooler on her hands trying to make an impression. "Lots of times when kids are on a visit," Pavon said, "they don't say a word." Not Smith.

VOLUNTEERS

"She was saying how far she could hit it. We were saying, 'Yeah, whatever.'"

But when Smith pulled out her driver, stepped up to the tee, and blasted away, all notions of bragging were immediately dispelled. She wasn't boasting; she was simply stating a fact.

Mankind is forever busy with his achievements and his progress. Cars, planes, computers, Ipods, Oreos. We have been to the moon, virtually eliminated polio, built a tunnel from England to France, concocted weapons capable of destroying our planet, and come up with the flush toilet, chicken nuggets, and Velcro.

We honor each other with prizes and awards for our accomplishments. We name buildings, highways, and bridges after folks who have achieved "great" things. As a species and as individuals, we do like to brag about what we've done,

The truth is, though, that we are nothing compared to God. We brag about space flight; God fashioned the moon, the planets, and the stars and hung them in the heavens he created. Man conducts a symphony; God directs the dawn. Man feebly predicts the weather; God commands it. We struggle to manage a business; God effortlessly manages the universe.

In truth, we have little of which to boast except that God loves us. Now that's worth bragging about!

Let the competition begin; let the glory be God's.
-- from the Fellowship of Christian Athletes Competitor's Creed

Boasting and bragging about ourselves
and our accomplishments is one sure way
to make God laugh.

CLOTHES HORSE

Read Genesis 37:1-11.

"Israel loved Joseph more than all his children, because he was the son of his old age: and he made him a coat of many colours" (v. 3 KJV).

Money was so tight in the early days of football at UT that uniforms were a hit-and-miss proposition.

Much about the beginnings of our nation's favorite sport were haphazard and rather primitive. For instance, the game had neither huddles nor time outs for anything except injuries. Since a player who left the game because of injury could not return, he was not removed "until at least two buckets of water, liberally sloshed over the fallen warrior, failed to bring him back to life and a desire for further combat."

Tennessee's football program constantly struggled with money worries. In 1899, some students bought an ad in the *Knoxville Sentinel* appealing for donations from alumni to keep the football team alive. The 1902 Vanderbilt game resulted in a net loss of $60.90; the Sewanee game the same year lost $15.80.

When North Carolina came to Knoxville in 1890, the expenses included $39.40 to board the team in a local hotel, $10 to advertise the game, a dollar to mark off the field, and 40 cents for buckets, a dipper, and chewing gum. Net loss for the game was $42.35.

Thus, the players had to scrimp and scrounge to pay for a team any way they could. Especially was this true of uniforms,

VOLUNTEERS

which pretty much didn't exist. The players wore jerseys, but "it was usually coincidence if any two of them matched." Stockings consisted of whatever the players could find and were of different colors. If a player had $1.25, he could buy himself some padded pants that featured leather shields at the shins and elbows.

In those early days, a football team certainly wasn't judged by the quality of the clothes it wore on the field.

On the other hand, contemporary society proclaims that it's all about the clothes. Buy that new suit or dress, those new shoes, and all the sparkling accessories, and you'll be a new person. The changes are only cosmetic, though; under those clothes, you're the same person. Consider Joseph, for instance, prancing about in his pretty new clothes; he was still a spoiled tattletale whom his brothers despised.

Jesus never taught that we should run around half-naked or wear only second-hand clothes from the local mission. He did warn us, though, against making consumer items such as clothes a priority in our lives. A follower of Christ seeks to emulate Jesus not through material, superficial means such as wearing special clothing like a robe and sandals. Rather, the disciple desires to match Jesus' inner beauty and serenity -- whether the clothes the Christian wears are the sables of a king or the rags of a pauper.

Equipment in the way of uniforms was doled out to the varsity. The Scrubs furnished their own.
                                    -- Football Player Benjamin White

**Where Jesus is concerned,
clothes don't make the person; faith does.**

SPREADING THE WORD

Read Mark 1:21-28.

"News about him spread quickly over the whole region"
(v. 28).

Tennessee's coaches were so desperate for a kicker, they ran advertisements. What they got was a dynasty.

In the early 1970s, the coach of Knoxville's South High School asked his team if anyone were interested in punting. "The entire team raised their hands," said the squad's star running back. "It kept getting narrowed down and I won the job." His name was Craig Colquitt.

After graduation in 1972, Colquitt drew interest from only Wofford and Lees-McRae. He wasn't enthusiastic about either, so he got a job in the china department at Miller's department store downtown and worked for two years. One day, though, he ran across a newspaper ad. Neil Clabo was a senior, and the Vols needed a punter; they were holding tryouts. Colquitt wrote George Cafego, UT's legendary kicking coach, and he said come on down. By the 1975 season-opener, Colquitt was the punter.

His first kick was a disaster. He attempted to punt from the end zone, but the snap "bounced off my chest and hit my face mask." He was smothered for a safety. Things got much better after that. Colquitt rewrote UT's record book by averaging 42.5 yards per punt for his career. He was All-SEC in 1976 and '77 and played in two Super Bowls for the Pittsburgh Steelers.

VOLUNTEERS

Today, though, Craig is only the fourth-best punter named Colquitt Tennessee has had. From 1981-84, his nephew, Jimmy, broke his records by averaging 43.9 yards for his career. Then came son Dustin, who bumped him to third place from 2001-05. His son Britton then knocked the old man down to fourth place from 2006-08. The top four punters in Volunteer history are all named Colquitt, and it all resulted from an ad in the paper.

Commercials and advertisements for products and services inundate us. Watch NASCAR: decals cover the cars and the drivers' uniforms. Turn on your computer: ads pop up. TV, radio, newspapers, billboards -- everyone's trying to get the word out the best way possible.

Jesus was no different in that he used the most effective and efficient means of advertising he had at his disposal to spread his message of salvation and hope among the masses. That was word of mouth. In his ministry, Jesus didn't isolate himself; instead, he moved from town to town among the common people, preaching, teaching, and healing. Those who encountered Jesus then told others about their experience, thus spreading the word about the good news.

Almost two millennia later, nothing's really changed. Speaking to someone else about Jesus remains the best way to get the word out, and the best advertisement of all is a changed life.

I feel like I've handed down a business to my sons.
-- Craig Colquitt on punting at UT

**The best advertising for Jesus is word of mouth,
telling others what he has done for you.**

DAY 77

A HOLLYWOOD ENDING

Read Luke 24:1-12.

"Why do you look for the living among the dead? He is not here; he has risen!" (vv. 5, 6a)

Even a Hollywood producer wouldn't touch this hokey story.

Here's the storyline. Coach tells player he's not good enough; player goes to new team; coach tells player he's not good enough; player comes in to lead one of greatest comebacks ever -- against his former team. Too corny to believe? It's Rick Clausen's story.

Clausen transferred to Tennessee in 2002 after being told at LSU that he wasn't good enough to play in the SEC. The week of the LSU game in 2005, coach Phillip Fulmer told him he wasn't good enough to start. But when the Vols met the fourth-ranked Tigers on Monday, Sept. 26, in a game delayed 48 hours by a hurricane, Tennessee's first half was as bad as the weather. The Vols trailed 21-0 and Fulmer put Clausen in.

What happened was "one of the greatest comebacks in UT football history." Clausen's 8-yard touchdown pass to wide receiver Bret Smith capped a 61-yard drive, but the Vols still trailed 24-7 heading into the last quarter. Clausen's one-yard sneak on fourth down ended a 75-yard drive that made it 24-14 with 9:35 to play. Three plays later cornerback Jonathan Hefney's interception and return set up a one-yard dive by Gerald Riggs. The UT defense held, Clausen led the offense to the Tiger 11, and James Wilhoit sent the game into overtime at 24 each with a 28-yard field goal.

LSU got a field goal on its possession. When Clausen hit Riggs to the 15, the impossible suddenly seemed probable. Riggs took it from there, scoring on third down from the one. UT had an improbable 30-27 win and Rick Clausen had an equally improbable Hollywood ending. For the night, the quarterback LSU didn't want was 21 for 32 for 196 yards and two touchdowns.

The world tells us that happy endings are for fairy tales and the movies, that reality is Cinderella dying in childbirth and her prince getting killed in a peasant uprising. But that's just another of the world's lies.

The truth is that Jesus Christ has been producing happy endings for almost two millennia. That's because in Jesus lies the power to change and to rescue a life no matter how desperate the situation. Jesus is the master at putting shattered lives back together, of healing broken hearts and broken relationships, of resurrecting lost dreams.

And as for living happily ever after – God really means it. The greatest Hollywood ending of them all was written on a Sunday morning centuries ago when Jesus left a tomb and death behind. With faith in Jesus, your life can have that same ending. You live with God in peace, joy, and love – forever. The End.

It was a tough week for myself. [My family] said you've got to stay because you never know what will happen.
-- Rick Clausen on the week of the 2005 LSU game

Hollywood's happy endings are products of imagination; the happy endings Jesus produces are real and are yours for the asking.

AUTHORITY FIGURE

Read Psalm 95:1-7a.

"Come, let us bow down in worship, let us kneel before the Lord" (v. 6).

Your head coach is an authority figure, so you do what he says, right? Scotty Hopson did, and the Volunteers had a last-minute basketball win over Florida.

On Sunday, Jan. 31, 2010, the 15-4 Vols hosted the 15-5 Gators in a key SEC matchup. "The game was won and lost on the boards," UT coach Bruce Pearl declared after it was all over. In the first half, though, it wasn't even a fair fight as the Gators outrebounded the Volunteers 20-14. Senior forward-center Wayne Chism, who finished with 16 points and 11 rebounds despite a sore knee, said it was a simple matter of being outnumbered. He and sophomore Renaldo Woolridge "were fighting five-on-two." Pearl made sure that problem got adjusted at halftime, and, said Chism, "In the second half, it was five-on-five down there trying to rebound, and you knew it was going to be a battle."

It was indeed. Down by six at halftime, Tennessee didn't take a last-half lead until the 12:17 mark. They had trailed for more than 25 minutes. Their biggest lead was five, and the Gators nailed a three to take a one-point lead in the final minute.

With 24.6 seconds left to play, Pearl called a time out and gave Hopson his instructions. The coach told the sophomore guard, "Win this for us." Hopson dutifully replied, "Yes, sir." Then he

VOLUNTEERS

went out and did it.

"When I got the ball, I took a dribble, pulled back, and had a look at the rim," Hopson recalled. "I shot it, and that's the last look I had." That's because he had a defender in his face, but "I just heard the reaction of the crowd, so I knew it went in." He then rebounded Florida's last-second shot and dribbled out the clock for the 61-60 Tennessee win.

Just like his coach told him to.

Stand up for yourself. Be your own person. Cherish your independence. That's what the world tells us. Naively, we may believe it and plan to live just that way – until we grow up and discover that authority figures don't take kindly to being challenged by those under their supervision or direction. Our basic survival skills kick in, and we change our tune: play along, don't rock the boat, be a company person. We become – gasp! – obedient, dampening our rebelliousness for a greater purpose.

Our relationship with God is similar in that he demands obedience from us. We believe in and trust what Jesus told us as the revealed word of God, and then we are obedient to it.

Obedience – even to God -- is not easy for us. It vexes us -- at least until we learn that what we surrender in independence to God is meaningless compared to the blessings we gain in return.

Football is like life; it requires perseverance, self-denial, hard work, sacrifice, dedication, and respect for authority.
                                                              – Vince Lombardi

**God seeks our obedience out of a loving desire to
provide us with rich, purposeful, and joyous lives.**

JUGGERNAUT

Read Revelation 20.

*"Fire came down from heaven and devoured them. And
the devil, who deceived them, was thrown into the lake of
burning sulfur, where the beast and the false prophet had
been thrown" (vv. 9b-10a).*

Most contemporary sports fans have short memory spans, but
the true fan of Tennessee football may well recall that the first
juggernaut the Vols ever fielded came way back in 1914.

89-0. 55-3. 66-0. 67-0. Those were just some of the scores the 1914
squad rolled up on the way to a 9-0 record, the school's first true
undefeated season, and its first-ever conference championship.
(The 1896 squad went 4-0 against mostly inferior competition.)
Most importantly, they beat both Alabama and Vanderbilt.

Until that 1914 season, the Vols were pretty mediocre. Since the
program's inception in 1891, they had lost to Alabama eight times
and had not defeated Vanderbilt in twelve tries.

In 1911, Z.G. Clevenger, who had coached since 1907 at Nebraska
Wesleyan, was hired as Tennessee's head football coach. "There
was nothing attractive about football," he once said. "The only
players were those with an intense desire to play." Long before
Gen. Robert Neyland rendered the single wing synonymous with
Tennessee football, Clevenger used the T formation. His 1914
squad buried Carson-Newman 89-0 in the opener, and by the
time 3-0 Alabama rolled into Knoxville, the Vols were 4-0 and

had outscored their opponents 237-3.

The season before, Alabama had recorded its seventh straight shutout of the Vols 6-0 in a wild game finished in the dark with the aid of spectators' car headlights. In 1914, the juggernaut Vols won 17-7. They then whipped Chattanooga to set up "the most talked-about and long-awaited game in Tennessee's history." Alonzo M. "Goat" Carroll almost singlehandedly beat Vandy 16-14. He scored all of UT's points on a pair of touchdown passes from Bill May, an extra point, and a 15-yard field goal.

Maybe your experience with a juggernaut involved a game against a team full of major college prospects, a league tennis match against a former college player, or your presentation for the project you knew didn't stand a chance. Whatever it was, you've been slam-dunked before.

Being part of a juggernaut is certainly more fun than being in the way of one. Just consider UT's opponents in 1914. Or consider the forces of evil aligned against God. At least the teams that took the field against the 1914 Vols had some hope, however slim, that they might win. No such hope exists for those who oppose God.

That's because their fate is already spelled out in detail. It's in the book; we all know how the story ends. God's enemies may talk big and bluster now, but they will be trounced in the most decisive defeat of all time.

You sure want to be on the winning side in that one.

"Next year" was here at last.

-- Sportswriter Russ Bebb on the 1914 football season

**The most lopsided victory in all of history
is a sure thing: God's ultimate triumph over evil.**

DAY 80

HEAD GAMES

Read Job 28.

"The fear of the Lord -- that is wisdom, and to shun evil is understanding" (v. 28).

Legendary UT coach Bob Neyland was a master at using his head to get inside others' heads.

For instance, before the 1946 game at Boston College, the General told his team they were poorly prepared to defend the Eagles because of their T formation. He said BC would probably run all up and down the field the first half, but the team shouldn't be too bothered by it, that they'd be ready for the third quarter.

Sure enough, Boston College scored twice in the first quarter, but the Volunteers settled down and caught on to the newfangled offense. Tennessee trailed only 13-7 at halftime. Neyland then proceeded to get inside the Eagles' helmets. When the first half ended, he told line coach Murray Warmath "to yell and run toward the dressing room." Warmath said his boss then "gave a blood-curdling scream and we all took off. Our players went storming for the tunnel," right past "the tired, sweaty Boston College players. . . . You should have seen the expressions on their faces." Tennessee won 33-13.

Neyland often used head games on his own team too. In the fourth quarter of the 1951 Cotton Bowl against favored Texas, the Vols drove 83 yards for a touchdown. But tailback Pat Shires missed the extra point that would have tied the game. He trotted dejectedly to the bench with tears streaming down his face. His coach, legendary for his military discipline, came over and put a comforting arm around his player. Then being sure he spoke loudly enough for his team to hear, he said, "Don't worry about that, son. We didn't come down here to tie."

Hope rekindled, defensive back Jimmy Hill recovered a fumble and fullback Andy Kozar scored for the 20-14 upset.

You're a thinking person. When you talk about using your head, you're speaking as Gen. Neyland illustrated repeatedly in his career: Logic and reason are part of your psyche. A coach's bad call frustrates you and your children's inexplicable behavior flummoxes you. Why can't people just think things through?

That goes for matters of faith too. Jesus doesn't tell you to turn your brain off when you walk into a church or open the Bible. In fact, when you seek Jesus, you seek him heart, soul, body, and mind. The mind of the master should be the master of your mind so that you consider every situation in your life through the critical lens of the mind of Christ. With your head *and* your heart, you encounter God, who is, after all, the true source of wisdom.

To know Jesus is not to stop thinking; it is to start thinking divinely.

When this game's over with, they'll be playing the 'Tennessee Waltz.'
-- Bob Neyland to his players prior to the 1951 Cotton Bowl when the
Texas band played 'The Eyes of Texas Are Upon You'

Since God is the source of all wisdom,
it's only logical that you encounter him
with your mind as well as your emotions.

DAY 81

KNOW-IT-ALLS

Read Matthew 13:10-17.

"The knowledge of the secrets of the kingdom of heaven has been given to you" (v. 11).

Tennessee's new women's basketball coach had a rather embarrassing secret: She knew absolutely nothing about the game.

Margaret Hutson was 32 years old when she succeeded Joan Cronan as head coach of the Lady Vols in 1970. "Except for participating in a few church league outings and overseeing a loosely organized prep school team, she was a virtual stranger" to basketball.

Thus, she was rather anxious when she met with "a motley crew of sixty walk-on candidates" for the team. She managed to make it through the meeting with her secret undiscovered, but was then met by a player who asked her a question: "Coach, are we going to play pattern or freelance?" Hutson had no idea what the girl was talking about. She decided to bluff, replying, "It will depend on what our personnel will be." Apparently satisfied, the player nodded and left, and Hutson breathed a big sigh of relief.

The basketball team was an afterthought in the first place. She was hired as a PE instructor and then told, "By the way, you'll be coaching women's basketball." The job was so incidental it wasn't worth the bother of a press release, a contract, or a handshake.

She embarked on a crash course to learn the game. She read books, deluged men's assistant coach Stu Aberdeen with questions, and attended a number of coaching camps, including one at which one of the counselors was a player named Pat Head.

Hutson learned well. She won 60 games in her four seasons as coach and has the second-highest winning percentage in school history, behind only the coach who succeeded her, that former camp counselor who's still on the job.

We can never know too much. We once thought our formal education ended when we entered the workplace, but now we have constant training sessions, conferences, and seminars to keep us current whether our expertise is in auto mechanics or medicine. Many areas require graduate degrees now as we scramble to stay abreast of new discoveries and information. And still we never know it all.

Nowhere, however, is the paucity of our knowledge more stark than it is when we consider God. We will never know even a fraction of all there is to apprehend about the creator of the universe – with one important exception. God has revealed all we need to know about the kingdom of heaven to ensure our salvation. He has opened to us great and eternal secrets.

All we need to know about getting into Heaven is right there in the Bible. With God, ignorance is no excuse and knowledge is salvation.

If lessons are learned in defeat, our team is getting a great education.
– UT Assistant and Minnesota Head Football Coach Murray Warmath

When it comes to our salvation, we can indeed know it all because God has revealed to us everything we need to know.

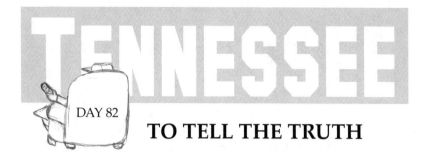

DAY 82

TO TELL THE TRUTH

Read Matthew 5:33-37.

*"Simply let your 'Yes' be 'Yes,' and your 'No,' 'No';
anything beyond this comes from the evil one" (v. 37).*

Because Bear Bryant and Bill Battle both told the truth, the Vols landed one of their most celebrated and exciting players ever.

Condredge Holloway led Tennessee in total offense for three straight seasons (1972-74). "The Artful Dodger" probably is still best known for his scrambling ability, but he ended his career with the best interception-to-attempts ratio in school history. He threw only twelve interceptions in 407 attempts. He is a member of eight halls of fame, including the Canadian Football Hall of Fame and the Tennessee Sports Hall of Fame.

As a senior in high school, Holloway "was arguably the most sought-after athlete in America." In addition to his obvious football skills, he could have played basketball for UCLA and coach John Wooden and could have signed a pro baseball contract with the Montreal Expos. When his mother nixed his bypassing college to play pro ball, he decided on football.

Alabama was the obvious choice for the Huntsville youngster, and the Tide was interested. On a recruiting visit, though, the Bear told the truth when Holloway asked him if he could play quarterback. "No," was Bryant's answer. "We're not ready for this." "This" was a black quarterback.

Holloway respected Bryant for his truthfulness. "What Coach

VOLUNTEERS

Bryant did was big in my book," he said. He understood that Bryant could have lied and then have put him in the defensive backfield. "What am I going to say?" Holloway asked. "Am I going to call a legendary coach a liar, me, a 17-year-old kid?"

Tennessee recruited well too, and when Holloway asked head coach Bill Battle the same question he'd asked Bryant, he again got a truthful answer. Battle "told me if I was good enough, I could play quarterback." That clinched it. Holloway was certainly good enough, and he became the SEC's first black quarterback.

No, that dress doesn't make you look fat. But, officer, I wasn't speeding. I didn't get the project finished because I've been at the hospital every night with my ailing grandmother. What good-looking guy? I didn't notice.

Sometimes we lie to spare the feelings of others; more often, though, we lie to bail ourselves out of a jam, to make ourselves look better to others, or to gain the upper hand over someone.

But Jesus admonishes us to tell the truth. Frequently in our faith life we fret about what is right and what is wrong, but we can have no such ambivalence when it comes to telling the truth or lying. God and his son are so closely associated with the truth that lying is ultimately attributed to the devil ("the evil one"). Given his character, God cannot lie; given his character, the devil lies as a way of life. Given your character, which is it?

Being a Volunteer is about the people who told you the truth when you got there and told you the truth four years later when you left.
-- Condredge Holloway

Jesus declared himself to be the truth,
so whose side are we on when we lie?

BELIEVE IT!

Read John 3:16-21.

"For God so loved the world that He gave His only begotten Son, that whoever believes in Him should not perish but have everlasting life" (v. 16 NKJV).

According to all the so-called experts, the Volunteers were about to get whipped soundly. The Orange Nation apparently didn't believe a word of it.

On Jan. 1, 1986, Tennessee met Miami in the Sugar Bowl. The Hurricanes were ranked second in the nation while the Vols had a loss and two ties besmirching their record. The experts took one look at the respective rosters and realized that "the game appeared to be a colossal mismatch." A future Heisman-Trophy winner quarterbacked the Canes; second-stringer Daryl Dickey led the Volunteers. Expectations of a massacre should have been enough to keep Tennessee fans out of New Orleans. And yet, they showed up in droves; they believed.

So did their team. What happened in the 1986 Sugar Bowl had to be seen to be believed as the Vols played a near-perfect game to put a "mind-boggling" 35-7 whipping on Miami. The margin of the win has been topped in Vol bowl history only by the 38-7 blowout of Texas A&M in the 2005 Cotton Bowl.

The game started out just as everyone believed it would when Miami took an early 7-0 lead. After that, well, just believe it. First, Dickey hit tight end Jeff Smith on a 6-yard touchdown pass in the second quarter. Then receiver Tim McGee recovered a fumble in the end zone to give the Vols a surprising 14-7 halftime lead.

It got better -- or more unbelievable if you will. Fullback Sam Henderson's 1-yard run made it 21-7. Track man Jeff Powell raced 60 yards for another score only moments later, and Charles Wilson completed the slaughter with a 6-yard TD in the final quarter.

When the rout was over, everybody believed in the Vols.

What we believe underscores everything about our lives. Our politics. How we raise our children. How we treat other people. Whether we respect others, their property and their lives.

Often, competing belief systems clamor for our attention; we all know persons – maybe friends and family members – who lost Christianity in the shuffle and the hubbub. We turn aside from believing in Christ at our peril, however, because the heart and soul, the very essence of Christianity, is belief. That is, believing that this man named Jesus is the very Son of God and that it is through him – and only through him – that we can find forgiveness and salvation that will reserve a place for us with God.

But believing is more than simply acknowledging intellectually that Jesus is God. Even the demons who serve Satan know that. It is belief so deep that we entrust our lives and our eternity to Christ. We live like we believe it – because we do.

This evening belonged to an always-believing band of Volunteers.
                    -- Writer Randy Moore on the win over Miami

**Believe it: Jesus is the way – and the only way
– to eternal life with God.**

REVELATION

Read Isaiah 53.

*"But he was pierced for our transgressions, he was
crushed for our iniquities; the punishment that brought
us peace was upon him, and by his wounds we are healed"
(v. 5).*

In 1968, a pioneer in women's sports at UT took a look into the future and discerned quite correctly what was coming. She didn't want to be a part of it, and so she stepped aside.

The growth of women's athletics at UT was inevitable, but the origins of the programs really cannot be imagined without Nancy Lay. In 1960, Lay, a graduate student, reestablished UT's women's basketball program. Until 1968, she and physical education instructor Jo Hobson shared the coaching duties for the three women's sports: basketball, tennis, and volleyball.

She had no athletic scholarships. Her heftiest budget for the basketball team was $500. The teams comprised primarily physical education majors and competed mainly against nearby schools. Volleyball pioneer Deb Dyer (Handy) remembered that anyone could try out simply by signing up. The players would pile into six or eight cars for road trips, helping to pay for the gas and staying in dorms. Once as awards for "winning a tournament or something like that," Lay handed out toenail clippers to the participants. "They were like a hundred for a dollar," she said.

In the late 1960s, attitudes about women's collegiate sports began to change, leading to increased funding and more widespread competition. That's when Lay saw a new day dawning for women's basketball, a time when it would be big-time athletics. She was a teacher first and didn't want to be a full-time head coach so she resigned. She served several years as UT's coordinator of women's sports, envisioning another future in 1974 by helping to hire Pat Head as women's basketball coach.

In our jaded age, we have relegated prophecy to dark rooms where mysterious women peer into crystal balls or clasp our sweaty palms while uttering vague generalities. At best, we understand a prophet as someone who predicts or foresees future events or trends as Nancy Lay did.

When we open the pages of the Bible, though, we encounter something radically different. A prophet is a messenger from God, one who relays divine revelation to others.

Prophets seem somewhat foreign to us because in one very real sense the age of prophecy is over. In the name of Jesus, we have access to God through our prayers and through scripture. In searching for God's will for our lives, we seek divine revelation. We may speak only for ourselves and not for the greater body of Christ, but we do not need a prophet to discern what God would have us do. We need faith in the one whose birth, life, and death fulfilled more than 300 Bible prophecies.

I knew what was coming.
-- Nancy Lay in 1968 on the future of women's collegiate sports

**Persons of faith continuously
seek a word from God for their lives.**

DAY 85

TEAM PLAYERS

Read 1 Corinthians 12:4-13; 27-31.

"Now to each one the manifestation of the Spirit is given for the common good" (v. 7).

When Paul Brown was assembling an expansion franchise in Cincinnati in 1968, the first player he ever drafted was a Volunteer. He was taken not because of the position he played but because of how he played it and the fact that he was the ultimate team player.

A quarterback or a dominant defensive player -- those are the positions conventional wisdom says you corral first when you're putting together a new team. But Brown drafted -- of all things -- a center because that center was Bob Johnson. From 1965-67, Johnson was a two-time All-America who won the Jacobs Trophy in 1967 as the SEC's best blocker. He even finished sixth in the Heisman Trophy voting. Eventually, he would be named to the all-time All-SEC team and in 1989 would be elected to the College Football Hall of Fame.

More than his ability, however -- which indeed was daunting -- Johnson succeeded because of his leadership skills and his team mentality. UT line coach Ray Trail said Johnson wasn't the rah-rah type but led rather by example. "He went to church," Trail said. "He was a good person, the kind you'd be proud to call your friend." Reggie Jellicorse, the starting center in 1965 until an injury moved Johnson into the lineup for good, called Johnson,

VOLUNTEERS

"a good player, a good student, a good man, a good Christian."

Consistent with his approach, Johnson took his personal fame in stride because most of all he liked UT's 25-6-2 record while he played. He never sought out headlines, stating that trophies and plaques "are often based on what others say about you. Winning was based on what he and teammates did."

Most accomplishments are the result of teamwork, whether it's a college football team, the running of a household, the completion of a project at work, or a dance recital. Disparate talents and gifts work together for the common good and the greater goal.

A church works exactly the same way. At its most basic, a church is a team assembled by God. A shared faith drives the team members and impels them toward shared goals. As a successful Tennessee team must have running backs and offensive tackles -- a dominating center also helps -- so must a church be composed of people with different spiritual and personal gifts. The result is something greater than everyone involved.

What makes a church team different from others is that the individual efforts are expended for the glory of God and not self. The nature of a church member's particular talents doesn't matter; what does matter is that those talents are used as part of God's team.

What the heck is a Bengal?
                    — Bob Johnson's wife, Jane, on draft day 1968

A church is a team of people
using their various talents and gifts for God,
the source of all those abilities to begin with.

NOT WHAT THEY SEEM

Read Habakkuk 1:2-11.

"Why do you make me look at injustice? Why do you tolerate wrong? Destruction and violence are before me; there is strife, and conflict abounds" (v. 3).

When Ron Slay played, things on the basketball court weren't always what they seemed. Just ask Louisiana-Lafayette.

Slay was once described as "a bona fide flake." He showed up for his first practice in 1999 wearing a mask like those in the horror movie *Scream*. "Slay played flamboyantly, talked incessantly, and clowned constantly." While Slay's antics may have captured the attention of his opponents, behind them was a talented basketball player. As a senior in 2002-03, Slay was the SEC Player of the Year and first-team All-SEC.

As the sixth man, freshman Slay was a key component of the 1999-2000 squad, which set a school record for the time with 24 regular-season wins. In the opening round of the NCAA tournament against Louisiana-Lafayette, Slay's "all-out effort, coupled with his zany antics, had the [opposing] players befuddled. 'Sometimes,' Slay said, 'they looked at me like I wanted to bite 'em or something.'"

Slay's propensity for unpredictable on-court antics came into play with only 13.3 seconds left in that game. He had scored 11 points in a Volunteer surge into the lead at 60-58. He snared an offensive rebound, was bumped as he went back up, and "crashed awkwardly to the floor, grimacing in pain. He remained there while teammates gathered around and officials assessed the damage." Considering the "brutality of the assault," the officials had to rule the foul was flagrant, which gave the Vols two free throws and possession. Tennessee won 63-58.

When the game ended, Slay "apparently blessed with miraculous recuperative powers -- bounded around the arena in a typically uninhibited celebration." His brutal injury was faked.

Sometimes in life -- as in basketball -- things aren't what they seem. In our violent and convulsive times, we must confront the possibility of a new reality: that we are helpless in the face of anarchy; that injustice, destruction, and violence are pandemic in and symptomatic of our modern age. It seems that anarchy is winning, that the system of standards, values, and institutions we have cherished is crumbling while we watch.

But we should not be deceived or disheartened. God is in fact the arch-enemy of chaos, the creator of order and goodness and the architect of all of history. God is in control. We often misinterpret history as the record of mankind's accomplishments -- which it isn't -- rather than the unfolding of God's plan -- which it is. That plan has a clearly defined end: God will make everything right. In that day things will be what they seem.

I was working on my Oscar performance for later this year.
    -- Ron Slay, when asked if he were hurt in the UL-Lafayette game

**The forces of good and decency often seem
helpless before evil's power, but don't be fooled:
God is in control and will set things right.**

NIGHTFALL

Read Psalm 68:12-23.

"The day is yours, and yours also the night; you established the sun and moon" (v. 16).

Alan Duncan didn't want to return to Africa after he attended the first night football game in Neyland Stadium history.

Football began at what was then Shields-Watkins Field in 1921 with a 27-0 trouncing of Emory and Lee. Not until Sept. 16, 1972, though, did the Vols play there under the lights, a 28-21 win over Penn State. Duncan, a 13-year-old high-school soccer player, was in the stands that night.

At the time, Duncan and his family were in Knoxville on furlough from their missionary work in Kenya. What impressed young Duncan the most that fateful night was Vol barefoot kicker Ricky Townsend and the crowd's enthusiastic cheers when he was good on his kicks. "I bet I can do that," the teenager thought. "From that point, I set my sights on kicking for the Vols."

He declared he was staying in Tennessee rather than returning to Africa with the family. His dad would have none of it: "Son, I believe it's the Lord's will that we stay together as a family." Who can argue with Dad and the Lord? Duncan returned to Africa. As he grew up and matured, the teenager realized God had called him to spend his own life in service as a missionary.

But he never got over the impression that one night game had made on him. He wrote UT Coach Bill Battle asking for a scholarship; Battle replied that Duncan could try out for the team as a walk-on. "That was all the encouragement I needed," Duncan said. He arrived at UT in August of 1976 and earned the junior varsity starting placekicking position. He went on to lead the team in scoring three years running, wound up fifth on the all-time UT scoring list, set the school record for most consecutive extra points in a season, and was second-team All-SEC as a senior in 1980. In the 29-14 win over Kentucky in 1978, he scored 17 points, the school record for most points by a kicker in a game.

A rarity in the early days of the game, night football has become an accepted part of contemporary college football. With the lighting expertise we have today, our night games are played under conditions that are "as bright as day."

It is artificial light, though, man-made, not God-made. Our electric lights can only illumine a portion of God's night; they can never chase it away. The night, like the day, is a gift from God to be enjoyed, to function as a necessary part of our lives. The night is a part of God's plan for creation and a natural cycle that includes activity and rest.

The world is different at nightfall. Whether we admire a stunning sunset, are dazzled by fireflies, or simply find solace in the descending quiet, the night reminds us of the variety of God's creation and the need the creation has for constant renewal.

I don't like night games. It gets late too early.

-- Yogi Berra

**Like the day, night is part of both
the beauty and the order of God's creation.**

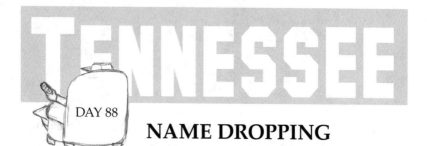

NAME DROPPING

Read Exodus 3:13-20.

*"God said to Moses, 'I AM WHO I AM. This is what
you are to say to the Israelites: 'I AM has sent me to you'"*
(v. 14).

The football season of 1905 was a pretty dreary one for the
Orange and White except for one very significant event: The team
acquired a nickname.

Tennessee's football squad went 3-5-1. The wins were not
exactly against big-time competition: the Tennessee School for
the Deaf, American University, and the Centre College Praying
Colonels. The game against American was noteworthy in that
Tennessee won 104-0, the school scoring record for a single game.
In the 11-6 loss to Sewanee, Sam McAllester notched UT's score
with a 107-yard return of a fumble. He had gained some fame
the season before in a win over Alabama when Coach S.D. "Sax"
Crawford had a belt with handles sewn into McAllester's uniform.
His teammates then catapulted him over the line.

The 1905 team was the first one to play as the "Volunteers."
In the spring, that nickname first appeared in local newspapers
though the team had been referred to off and on as "the Volunteer
State boys" since 1897. The *Atlanta Constitution* had called the team
the "Volunteers' in a 1902 article.

The nickname, of course, had its beginnings long before the
university began playing football. Large numbers of Tennesseans

VOLUNTEERS

volunteered for the War of 1812, and they again showed their readiness to volunteer with the Mexican War of 1846-48. When Gov. Aaron V. Brown issued a call for 2,800 men to serve in that conflict, 30,000 Tennessee men responded. The state itself became known as the "Volunteer State," and the UT nickname almost inevitably followed.

Nicknames such as the Volunteers are not slapped haphazardly upon individuals but rather reflect widely held perceptions about the person named. Proper names do that also.

Nowhere throughout history has this concept been more prevalent than in the Bible, where a name is not a mere label but is an expression of the essential nature of the named one. That is, a person's name reveals his or her character. Even God shares this concept; to know the name of God is to know God as he has chosen to reveal himself to us.

What does your name say about you? Honest, trustworthy, a seeker of the truth and a person of God? Or does the mention of your name cause your coworkers to whisper snide remarks, your neighbors to roll their eyes, or your friends to start making allowances for you?

Most importantly, what does your name say about you to God? He, too, knows you by name.

One of the admirers of the old school has suggested "the Volunteers." The name sounds good, and it is likely that it will stick.
-- Knoxville Journal *in 1905 on UT's nickname*

**Live so that your name evokes
positive associations by people you know,
by the public, and by God.**

DAY 89

LESSON LEARNED

Read Psalm 143.

"Teach me to do your will, for you are my God" (v. 10).

By the time she let Knoxville, Daedra Charles was a two-time All America who won the Wade Trophy as the best player in the country. First, though, she had to learn a thing or two about being a Volunteer.

A dominant 6-foot-3 center from Detroit, Charles played for Tennessee from 1988-91 and led the team to a national title in 1991. She was the SEC Woman Athlete of the Year that season and would eventually have her No. 32 retired, one of only five Lady Vol players so honored. She was on the 1992 Olympic team.

In the light of hindsight, it's difficult to believe that Pat Summitt and her coaches had severe doubts about Charles when she was a freshman, but they did. For one thing, she "had a somewhat lacka-daisical attitude toward attending class. She figured that since she was now in college, as long as she did the work everything would be fine." Maybe, but not with Summitt and her no-tolerance policy on skipping class.

A Proposition 48 student, which rendered her academically ineligible for basketball her freshman year, Charles skipped a class one day. She was blissfully unaware that Summitt had standing instructions that all her players' professors were to call her immediately if anyone missed even a single class.

So Charles was summoned to Summitt's office. The coach

VOLUNTEERS

recalled that she "smiled pleasantly, waved her to a chair, and said, 'Sit down.'" Then she dropped the bomb on her unsuspecting truant: "What gives you the right to skip class?" Charles just sat there. Summitt said she "could literally see those words pass through her mind, *How does she know?*" Summitt then ordered Charles to a series of grueling 5 a.m. runs.

Charles never skipped class again and graduated in four years with a degree in child and family studies. Lesson learned.

Learning about anything in life requires a combination of education and experience. Education is the accumulation of facts that we call knowledge; experience is the acquisition of wisdom and discernment, which add purpose and understanding to our knowledge.

The most difficult way to learn is trial and error: dive in blindly and mess up. The best way to learn is through example coupled with a set of instructions: Someone shows you the way and has written down all the information you need to follow.

In teaching us the way to live godly lives, God chose the latter method. He set down in his book the habits, actions, and attitudes that make for a way of life in accordance with his wishes. He also sent us Jesus to explain and to illustrate.

God teaches us not just how to exist but how to live. We just need to be attentive students.

The lessons learned upon the football field are carried usefully on to the field of life.

– Gen. Robert Neyland

**To learn from Jesus is to learn what life
is all about and how God means for us to live it.**

TOP SECRET

Read Romans 2:1-16.

"This will take place on the day when God will judge
men's secrets through Jesus Christ, as my gospel declares"
(v. 16).

As they marched toward the 1998 national championship, the Tennessee football team had a secret that helped keep them undefeated. It was a stick.

Like all other head football coaches, Phillip Fulmer was always looking for innovative ways to motivate his team and help keep them focused. The week before the Bama game, a good friend sent Fulmer, an avid hiker, a walking stick with his name and "Tennessee Vols" carved on it. Fulmer took the stick with him to practice "just to show the players and as a conversation piece." The players got a kick out of it, laughing that Fulmer looked like Moses walking around with his staff.

That night Fulmer suddenly realized how apt the Moses image was in that Moses had led his people to the Promised Land. Fulmer admitted to himself that what he had in mind "seemed a little crazy," but the team "needed a charge for the run during the last half of the season."

So, walking stick in hand, he gathered the team the next day and told them he would lead them to the promised land of an undefeated season and the stick would be their Synergy Stick. Every time they saw it, they would be reminded that the focus of their energy was on winning the next game. It would recharge and refocus them to give their best effort. And the stick was to be their secret. "It's just for us. Can't tell your girlfriend, your parents, the media, no one. The synergy is not to be shared," Fulmer said.

The players bought into Fulmer's sincerity, and the stick went everywhere after that. "One player carried it with pride and our players made it work," the coach said. With the team's secret in hand, Fulmer knew right then they would win them all.

As with the Vols and their synergy stick, we all have secrets we prefer to keep to ourselves. Nowadays, that requires increased vigilance on our part. Much information about us -- from credit reports to what movies we rent -- is readily available to prying and persistent persons. In our information age, people we don't know may know a lot about us — or at least they can find out. And some of them may use this information for harm.

While diligence may allow us to be reasonably successful in keeping some secrets from the world at large, we should never deceive ourselves into believing we are keeping secrets from God. God knows everything about us, including the things we wouldn't want proclaimed at church. All our sins, mistakes, failures, short-comings, quirks, prejudices, and desires – God knows all our would-be secrets.

But here's something God hasn't kept a secret: No matter what he knows about us, he loves us still.

Is this corny or what?.
– Phillip Fulmer's thought as he explained the walking stick to his team

We have no secrets before God, and it's no secret that he nevertheless loves us still.

NOTES
(by Devotion Day Number)

1   H.K. Denlinger, who had played . . . obtain a foothold here,": Russ Bebb, *The Big Orange* (Huntsville, AL: The Strode Publishers, 1973), p. 24.

1   "If we are routed in . . . to balance up accounts.": Bebb, p. 25.

1   Honeyman missed out on . . . bitten by a spider.: Bebb, pp. 24-25.

1   History recorded ten names . . . lost for the ages.: Bebb, p. 25.

1   "About one hundred people . . . boys took in the theater.": Bebb, p. 26.

1   Football is a comparatively new . . . think they will win.: Bebb, p. 25.

2   "school's most famous football . . . a big fundraising campaign.: Marvin West, *Legends of the Tennessee Vols* (Champaign, IL: Sports Publishing L.L.C., 2005), p. 24.

2   "everybody though [Peyton would] follow the leader to Ole Miss.": West, *Legends of the Tennessee Vols*, p. 24.

2   "they decided early that . . . an influence" on Peyton's decision.: West, *Legends of the Tennessee Vols*, p. 24.

2   When it came time for . . . He said it was Tennessee.": West, *Legends of the Tennessee Vols*, p. 25.

2   You pray a lot, and you just know what you're going to do.: Marvin West, *Tales of the Tennessee Vols* (Champaign, IL: Sports Publishing L.L.C., 2001), p. 17.

3   He coined the phrase . . . Roger Peltz on a unicycle.: John Adams, "Mears 'Lived for a Good Battle,'" *The Knoxville News-Sentinel*, June 12, 2007.

3   "after a few whiffs of oxygen . . . crowd of about 2,500.: Tom Mattingly, "Sines Did Mears One Better, Scheduled Doubleheader," *The Knoxville News-Sentinel*, Dec. 7, 2008.

3   I did wake up . . . they wanted to call it off.: Mattingly.

4   Neyland said his team was lucky . . . a seat on the bench.: Bob Gilbert, *Neyland* (Savannah: Golden Coast Publishing Company, 1990), p. 184.

4   The source of the ruckus . . . get him off the field.": Gilbert, p. 185.

5   "an almost illusory passing . . . flicker around the court.": Pat Summitt with Sally Jenkins, *Raise the Roof* (New York: Broadway Books, 1998), p. 5.

5   "a glamour girl," . . . brown hair and brown eyes.": Summitt, p. 86.

5   As the 1998 NCAA tournament . . . Summitt's office that day,: Summitt, p. 197.

5   Clement spotted the hair . . . at Summitt's expense.: Summitt, p. 198.

5   Ace Clement couldn't sit . . . of the football team.: Summitt, p. 86.

6   Some weak-of-heart Vol fans . . . the stadium's packed crowd.: Gary Lundy, "Vols Hog the Glory," *The Knoxville News-Sentinel*, Nov. 15, 1998.

6   were already crying, cursing . . . fall in the rankings.: John Adams, "Of Such Wins Are Championships Made," *The Knoxville News-Sentinel*, Nov. 15, 1998.

6   Defensive tackle Darwin Walker . . . off the ball so fast.": Adams, "Of Such Wins."

6   Our hopes, however, must be . . . disappointment, shame, and disaster.: P.S. Minear, "Hope," *The Interpreter's Dictionary of the Bible*, Vol. 2: E-J (Nashville: Abingdon Press, 1990), p. 641.

6   You've always got to have a shred of hope.: Adams, "Of Such Wins."

7   "set the modern standard . . . versatility, speed and fight.": "Vols Mourn Loss of Former All-America Tight End Denney," *UTSPORTS.COM*, Jan. 22, 2009, http://www.utsports.com/m-footbl-spec-rel/012209aaa.html, April 12, 2010.

7   "I think the kicker . . . to take the ball.": Mike Strange, "Denney Still Recalls How UT Faked out Syracuse in '66," *The Knoxville News-Sentinel*, Sept. 3, 1998.

7   Denney went over two Syracuse defenders: Strange, "Denney Still Recalls."

8   In the middle of her junior . . . all major college players in hitting: Debby Schriver, *In the Footsteps of Champions* (Knoxville: The University of Tennessee Press, 2008), p. 203.

8   Her mouth was wired shut . . . heart rate up.: Schriver, p. 203.

8   her teeth were clinched . . . it wasn't funny at all.": Schriver, p. 204.

8   "just healthy enough" to play,: Schriver, p. 203.

9   Ole Miss quarterback John . . . "God loves you, John.": West, *Legends of the Tennessee Vols*, p. 34.

9   "couldn't change the results, . . . happened as God's will.": West, *Legends of the Tennessee Vols*, p. 36.

9   he thought of becoming . . . . was its vice president.: West, *Legends of the Tennessee Vols*, p. 36.

9   He frequently stopped students on campus to witness to them,: West, *Legends of the Tennessee Vols*, pp. 36-37.

9   God gave Reggie White . . . for his very big heart.: West, *Legends of the Tennessee Vols*, p. 34.

10   In the spring of 1925, . . . Tennessee's new head coach.: West, *Legends of the Tennessee Vols*), p. 1.

10   "real beginning of Tennessee football,": West: *Legends of the Tennessee Vols*, p. 3.

10   The best move I ever made.: Chris Warner, *SEC Sports Quotes* (Baton Rouge: CEW Enterprises, 2002), p. 216.

11   "I cannot imagine anyone . . . a head coach at 22.": Dan Fleser, "Coaching Legend Still Grateful UT Took a Chance," *The Knoxville News-Sentinel*, March 23, 2005.

11   Summitt was courted as the graduate assistant.: Fleser, "Coaching Legend Still Grateful."

11   former coach Nancy Lay, the school's . . . she accepted Watson's proposal.: Randy Moore, *Hoop Tales: Tennessee Lady Volunteers* (Guilford, CN: The Globe Pequot Press, 2005), p. 57.

11   "I was jittery, . . . kind of jittery, too,": Jim Balloch, "Summitt Shoots for Record Book," *The Knoxville News-Sentinel*, March 22, 2005.

11   When Pat Summitt won her . . . the newspaper's game story.: Sam Venable, "Both Soared to Record Heights," *The Knoxville News-Sentinel*, March 24, 2005.

12   Growing up, Antone Davis . . . to eat the next day.: Ray Glier, *What It Means to Be a Volunteer* (Chicago: Triumph Books, 2008), p. 192-93.

12   "Manners were not at . . . Survival was at the top of my list.": Glier, p. 193.

12   "I pretty much got whatever . . . food on recruiting trips." Glier, p. 195.

12   "Coach Fulmer and I . . . under the sun.": Glier, p. 195.

12   when Davis arrived in . . . down to 299 pounds: Glier, p. 195.

13   Many still consider Reveiz . . . in UT football history.: Gus Manning and Haywood Harris, *Once a Vol, Always a Vol!* (Champaign, IL: Sports Publishing L.LC., 2006), p. 154.

13   In August 1981, head coach introduced Reveiz to Cafego,: Manning and Harris, p. 153.

13   "the most influential man . . . next to his grandfather.:

Manning and Harris, p. 154.

13   Cafego had no experience . . . "Your name is Frank.": Manning and Harris, p. 153.

13   For four years, Cafego . . . and earned his respect,": Manning and Harris, p. 154.

13   who had a veteran kicker . . . helped him make the team.: Manning and Harris, p. 158.

13   Coaches don't want to hear . . . holder or the snapper.: Manning and Harris, p. 158.

14   "I used my length,": David Climer, "Tennessee's J.P. Prince Defends Final Play Against Ohio State as Just a 'Clean Block,'" *The Tennessean*, March 27, 2010, http://pqasb.pqarchiver.com/tennessean/advancedsearch.html, April 16, 2010.

14   Prince had his instructions . . . Turner wherever he went.: David Climer, "Vols Have Earned Elite Status," *The Tennessean*, March 27, 2010, pqasb. pqarchiver.com/tennessean/advancedsearch.html, April 16, 2010.

14   "I'm just glad I . . . "It was a clean block.": Climer, "Vols Have Earned."

15   When we're between the lines, . . . person next to us.": Andy Staples, "Dooley Aiming to Salvage Messy Situation," *Sports Illustrated*, April 16, 2010, http://sportsillustrated.cnn.com/2010/writers/andy_staples/04/16/tennessee-dooley/index.html, April 17, 2010.

15   "Coach Dooley could leave . . . different position coaches.": Staples.

15   "more jaded than most 10-year NFL veterans.": Staples.

15   "had been through something . . . breach in trust.": Staples.

15   Dooley saw a good side . . . fight for each other.: Staples.

16   "I remember wondering . . . to score 80 or 85,": West, *Tales of the Tennessee Vols*, p. 46.

16   Majors jumped onto a training . . . "We're back in this thing.": West, *Tales of the Tennessee Vols*, p. 47.

16   Offensive coordinator Phillip Fulmer . . . made the perfect call.: West, *Tales of the Tennessee Vols*, p. 47.

16   Not in my lifetime and not at Notre Dame.: West, *Tales of the Tennessee Vols*, p. 47.

17   Women's basketball was pretty much . . . Cronan had no scholarships: Moore, *Hoop Tales: Tennessee Lady Volunteers*, p. 30.

17   an annual budget of $500.: Moore, *Hoop Tales: Tennessee Lady Volunteers*, p. 26.

17   "We were lucky if . . . people at our games.": Moore, *Hoop Tales: Tennessee Lady Volunteers*, p. 31.

17   they were playing in . . . didn't offer an orange uniform.: Moore, *Hoop Tales: Tennessee Lady Volunteers*, pp. 32, 35.

17   Cronan found some white . . . "I liked Carolina blue,": Moore, *Hoop Tales: Tennessee Lady Volunteers*, p. 35.

18   "We had some penalties and turnovers we didn't need,": Mike Strange, "Vols' Sub-Flub Pays Off," *The Knoxville News-Sentinel*, Nov. 3, 2002.

18   But guard Chavis Smith, . . . sprinted off the field.: Strange, "Vols' Sub-Flub."

18   It looked like a Chinese fire drill.: Strange, "Vols' Sub-Flub."

19   When he was nine, . . . intervention from local authorities.: West, *Legends of the Tennessee Vols*, p. 117.

19   Emanuel needed only two weeks . . . him into coming back.: West, *Legends of the Tennessee Vols*, p. 118.

19	"a spectacular neighborhood brawl" . . . stayed out of trouble.: West, *Legends of the Tennessee Vols*, p. 119.
19	He made 26 tackles, . . . led to a touchdown.: West, *Legends of the Tennessee Vols*, p. 120.
19	"despicable, vile, unprincipled scoundrels.": John MacArthur, *Twelve Ordinary Men* (Nashville: W Publishing Group, 2002), p. 152.
20	She called a time out to . . . "What's wrong with you?": Alan Ross, *Seven* (Nashville: Cumberland House, 2007), p. 77.
20	When Gordon said nothing, . . . she understood the message.: Ross, p. 78.
20	sank three straight shots: Ross, p. 78.
20	her star had taken . . . a root canal to save it.: Ross, p. 78.
20	That showed me Bridgette had it in her heart.: Ross, p. 78.
21	On a sunny summer day . . . town in West Virgina,: West, *Legends of the Tennessee Vols*, p. 46.
21	George Cafego always called it . . . 'I'll take care of you,'": West, *Legends of the Tennessee Vols*, p. 46.
21	His parents were dead,: West. *Legends of the Tennessee Vols*, p. 46.
21	he moved in with a . . . to feed and clothe me.": West, *Legends of the Tennessee Vols*, p. 48.
21	living with high-school coaches, . . . find a corner to sleep.": West, *Legends of the Tennessee Vols*, p. 46.
21	He had a borrowed suitcase . . . wouldn't have had them.: West, *Legends of the Tennessee Vols*, p. 48.
21	When Neyland decreed . . . suit and tie I ever owned.": West, *Legends of the Tennessee Vols*, p. 49.
22	"the greatest performance by . . . any time, any place.": Mike Strange, "Vols' 1980 Victory against Auburn Came from Nowhere," *The Knoxville News-Sentinel*, Oct. 1, 1998.
22	the largest home crowd . . . the worst home-field defeat: Strange, "Vols' 1980 Victory."
22	Before the team left . . . for a touchdown.": Strange, "Vols' 1980 Victory."
22	"General Custer among all these Indians.": Strange, "Vols' 1980 Victory."
22	We had some confidence . . . not anything like that.: Strange, "Vols' 1980 Victory."
23	"If we play the way . . . home a national championship.": Ross, p. 35.
23	a State forward, who, . . . "corn-fed chicks.": Ross, p. 36.
23	"Tennessee's corn-fed chicks had come home to roost": Ross, p. 44.
23	Tennessee had a stigma. . . . I couldn't stand it.: Ross, pp. 17-18.
24	Most of the recruiters . . . senior year of high school.: Chris Cawood, *Legacy of the Swamp Rat* (Kingston, TN: Magnolia Hill Press, 1994), p. 71.
24	In 1967, Wyche's best shot . . . Dewey Warren's backup.: Cawood, p. 73.
24	never having taken a snap . . . center Bob Johnson.: Cawood, p. 74.
24	Wyche's parents had missed . . . some extra spending money.: Cawood, p. 76.
24	The Alabama game was a . . . you can't find a seat.: Cawood, p. 80.
24	gave him one great hug.: Cawood, p. 80.
24	It was one sweet embrace.: Cawood, p. 80.
25	Bates never doubted he could make it in the pros.: Manning and Harris, p. 26.
25	He had long dreamed . . . outfits the Cowboys sported.: Manning and Harris, p. 24.
25	"I was pretty pumped up . . . he was unperturbed.: Manning

	and Harris, p. 26.
25	He determined NFL scouts . . . on the thirteenth round.: Manning and Harris, p. 26.
25	he noticed busloads . . . in the equipment room.: Manning and Harris, p. 27.
26	Coach [Ray] Mears never talked . . . just coach and player.": Mike Strange, "Robinson a Pioneer," *The Knoxville News-Sentinel*, Feb. 28, 2006.
26	"I didn't live in . . . squad for two seasons.: Strange, "Robinson a Pioneer."
26	Lloyd Richardson, who was . . . joy to be around.": Strange, "Robinson a Pioneer."
26	When I decided to . . . we were a team.: Strange, "Robinson a Pioneer."
27	recruiters invaded the family . . . "That's the one.": West, *Legends of the Tennessee Vols*, p. 99.
27	This was the first time . . . Shuler play in person.: Cawood, p. 215.
27	It was raining when . . . a reserve into giving him his.: Cawood, p. 215.
27	When he took the field . . . fifty yards that night," Cawood, p. 216.
28	"When people are going . . . we'll still be playing,": Gary Lundy, "Vols Adapt to Late-Night Kickoff in Different Ways," *The Knoxville News-Sentinel*, Oct. 15, 2004.
28	"I hate the late start," . . . want to see that stuff,": Lundy, "Vols Adapt."
28	I don't like it . . . twiddle your thumbs all day.: Lundy, "Vols Adapt."
29	The Lady Vols in January were in "near collapse.": Ross, p. 162.
29	"hang in there till next year.": Ross, p. 149.
29	she knew almost everybody . . . they weren't winning.: Ross, p. 149.
29	"hung in with their own private . . . fair to these kids.: Ross, p. 161.
29	If you had asked me . . . I'd have said you're crazy.: Ross, p. 161.
30	he sent a football film . . . not have major-college potential.: Glier, pp. 142-43.
30	He recalled that the coaches' . . . can't play offense, either.": Glier, p. 143.
30	He knew he wasn't . . . outwork everybody else.": Glier, p. 142.
30	"That No. 78 is as good as anybody I will see all year long.": Glier, 143.
31	followed blocks by Mike LaSorsa and Cotton Letner,: Randy Moore, *Stadium Stories: Tennessee Volunteers* (Guilford, CN: The Globe Pequot Press, 2004), p. 63.
31	The two-point conversion . . . nor defended one.: Moore, *Stadium Stories*, p. 64.
31	"We knew from the films . . . called the defense accordingly," Moore, *Stadium Stories*, p. 66.
31	We knew everything that LSU would do.: Moore, *Stadium Stories*, p. 70.
32	When he was 14, . . . after the game occurred.: Mike Strange, "Learning on the Run," *The Knoxville News-Sentinel*, Sept. 21. 2001.
33	Romans 5:3 is the foundation of the belief system that drives and shapes her.: Schriver, p. 216.
33	To remind her that . . . hope of Romans 5:3: Schriver, p. 216.
33	There are times when we suffer . . . and we can do it.: Schriver, 216.
34	that he frankly borrowed . . . coaches of the 1920s.: Gilbert, p. 5.
34	"One good blocker . . . The kicking game rules.": Gilbert, p. 4.
34	he was the first coach in the South . . . to release the ball.: Gilbert, p. 6.
35	A scout squad player once . . . back into the dining room.: West, *Legends of the Tennessee Vols*, p. 43.
35	It wasn't a good idea to take on Kiner.: West, *Legends of the Tennessee Vols*, p. 43.
36	"a game that began . . . but an enjoyable game.": Bebb, p. 58.

VOLUNTEERS

36   "After almost every down . . . the game was called,: Bebb, p. 58.

36   Almost every football game . . . to handle the crowd.: Bebb, p. 59.

37   Temple coach Don Casey saw . . . got a free throw at the end.: Mike Strange, "Night Crawler: Temple Set Stage in Knoxville for Time Clock," *The Knoxville News-Sentinel*, Nov. 8, 2007.

37   Tennessee fans pelted . . . lobby for a shot clock.: Strange, "Night Crawler."

37   It was so tight . . . point was important.: Strange, "Night Crawler."

38   every time center Bob Davis spit . . . cold to think about it.": Mike Strange, "In '50 Game, Vols Put Freeze on Wildcats' Dream of Title," *The Knoxville News-Sentinel*, Nov. 19, 1998.

38   The Vols had practiced . . . fumbled seven times.: Strange, "In '50 Game."

38   I'd come from Pennsylvania, . . . took the cake.: Strange, "In '50 Game."

39   "to strengthen weak ankles and increase their lung capacity.": Schriver, p. xxii.

39   "socially acceptable physical activities . . . after the 1926 season.: Schriver, p. xxii.

39   Hippity-hus! . . . the girls who play basket ball.: Schriver, p. xxiv.

40   "Friar Tuck in a high school production of *Robin Hood*.": West, *Legends of the Tennessee Vols*, p. 67.

40   Herman Hickman was 5-10 . . . balloon to 330 pounds.: West, *Legends of the Tennessee Vols*, p. 67.

40   NYU's most serious threat . . . *college football* had ever produced.: West, *Legends of the Tennessee Vols*, p. 69.

40   on the first staff at . . . "Hickman Picks Tech.": West, *Legends of the Tennessee Vols*, p. 71.

40   I can usually tell . . . going to be be up to par.: West, *Legends of the Tennessee Vols*, p. 70.

41   Come on, Dewey, . . . had his linemen singing.": West, *Legends of the Tennessee Vols*, p. 113.

41   Once he was late for . . . just like an old swamp rat.: West, *Legends of the Tennessee Vols*, p. 111.

41   "was slow as smoke.": West, *Legends of the Tennessee Vols*, p. 113.

41   "Warren jogged onto the field . . . didn't have his helmet.: West, *Legends of the Tennessee Vols*, p. 113.

41   to become the school's first pure passing quarterback.: Cawood, p. 54.

41   The blocking schemes weren't . . . "Come on Dewey, hum that tater.": West, Legends of the Tennessee Vols, p. 113.

42   Grunfeld was born of . . . settled in Forest Hills,: Randy Moore, *Hoop Tales: Tennessee Volunteers Men's Basketball* (Guilford, CN: The Globe Pequot Press, 2005), p. 89.

42   he got his hands . . . you'd better play basketball.": Moore, *Hoop Tales: Tennessee Volunteers Men's Basketball*, p. 89.

43   "Kevin exemplifies excellence,": John Adams, "From the Mean Streets to Monster Hits," *The Knoxville News-Sentinel*, Aug. 17, 2003.

43   The catalyst was the death . . . to do this again,": Adams, "From the Mean Streets."

43   Let me be an example . . . there is a better way.: Adams, "From the Mean Streets."

43   "a purely selfish matter . . . misfortune or frustration": Bruce T. Dahlberg, "Anger," *The Interpreter's Dictionary of the Bible* (Nashville: Abingdon Press, 1962), Vol. 1, p. 136.

TENNESSEE

44	"Alabama didn't punt . . . they had the chance.": Cawood, 127.
44	All I could see was the red flag in the corner.: Cawood, p. 128.
45	"a stunning performance.": John Adams, "For 11 Minutes, It Was Like Old Times for UT's Milligan," *The Knoxville News-Sentinel*, Feb. 23, 1998.
45	The team's orthopedist discovered . . . a strike for a layup.: Adams, "For 11 Minutes."
46	It's something that everyone always asks you.": Randy Kenner, "Never Too Late for UT Athletes to Graduate," *The Knoxville News-Sentinel*, Dec. 11, 2004.
46	After he left the university . . . spurred him to action.: Kenner.
46	he needed only some foreign . . . but I finally graduated.'": Kenner.
47	We had no superstars.": Moore, *Stadium Stories*, p. 147.
47	"I've been here nine years,. . . talented team we've had.: Moore, *Stadium Stories*, p. 146.
47	"It's the best team": Moore, *Stadium Stories*, p. 146.
47	"Not one of them cares . . . That's what's so special.": Moore, *Stadium Stories*, p. 147.
47	We lost all the superstars last year to the NFL." Moore, *Stadium Stories*, p. 147.
48	Lowery did not like to fly, . . . nearby all-night bakery.: West, *Tales of the Tennessee Vols*, p. 233.
48	"was the best back-to . . . ever had to this day.": Julian, Roland, "Widseth's Name, Numbers, Scary," *GoVolsXtra*, Jan. 5, 2008, http://www.govolsxtra. com/news/2008/jan/05/widseths-name-numbers-scary/, April 20, 2010.
48	"It was near midnight, . . . were already moving on,": West, *Tales of the Tennessee Vols*, p. 233.
48	Maybe we had lost our appetite.: West, *Tales of the Tennessee Vols*, p. 233.
49	When Professor Nathan D . . . the terrible series standings.": Bebb, p. 126.
49	"Vol hysteria was gripping . . . a record in the state.: Mike Strange, "'28 Vols Ended Domination by Beating Commodores," *The Knoxville News-Sentinel*, Nov. 23, 2000.
49	fell across the goal line as he was tackled.: Strange, "'28 Vols Ended."
50	abolishing football to concentrate . . . a 16-10 UT win.: Bebb, p. 29.
50	William B. Stokely . . . a football team in 1896.: Bebb, p. 29.
51	In 1947, Hank Lauricella was called . . . in both Knoxville and Oxford.: West, *Legends of the Tennessee Vols*, p. 63.
51	His first impression was . . . and run some plays.: West, *Legends of the Tennessee Vols*, p. 65.
51	"I really enjoyed myself," . . . and I said I did.": West, *Legends of the Tennessee Vols*, p. 65.
51	All these years later, I still love the University of Tennessee.: West, *Legends of the Tennessee Vols*, p. 65.
52	She was undecided about college . . . the orange dot up.: Schriver, p. 23.
52	she had no one to teach her . . . Brian Oldfield on TV.: Schriver, p. 23.
52	she was responsible . . . around her equipment.: Schriver, pp. 23-24.
52	Many people were looking . . . be cute doing that.': Schriver, p. 24.
53	Vol line coach Phillip Fulmer . . . his hand on a bat,": West, *Tales of the Tennessee Vols*, p. 107.
53	Jackson did a good job . . . much to do with that snake.": West, *Tales of the Tennessee Vols*, pp. 106-07.
53	I've been a lot of things, but never a snake-handler.: West, *Tales of the Tennessee Vols*, p. 107.

54 He could have quite literally . . . fell at the three.: Al Browning, *Third Saturday in October* (Nashville: Cumberland House, 2001), p. 362.

55 surgery required a dozen blades.: West, *Legends of the Tennessee Vols*, p. 91.

55 "I had to do something to relieve my frustration,": "Jack Reynolds, *Wikipedia, the free encyclopedia*, http://en.wikipedia.org/wiki/Jack_Reynolds_(American_football), March 11, 2010.

55 "Reynolds was a funny duck," . . . "but he's a good man.": West, *Legends of the Tennessee Vols*, p. 91.

55 Legendary UT Center Bob Johnson . . . warmups for agility drills.: West, *Legends of the Tennessee Vols*, p. 91.

55 "It happened every day," . . . a bizarre young man.": West, *Legends of the Tennessee Vols*, p. 93.

55 He relished the underdog . . . what he might do next.: West, *Legends of the Tennessee Vols*, p. 95.

55 Jack wasn't crazy; he was just different.: West, *Legends of the Tennessee Vols*, p. 91.

56 Bob Neyland followed his . . . three against the reserves.: Moore, *Stadium Stories*, p. 26.

56 "plowed into a small . . . and lost five yards.: Moore, *Stadium Stories*, p. 27.

56 I got in, but they pushed me back.: Moore, *Stadium Stories*, p. 27.

57 We weren't really into . . . had already been there.": Mike Strange, "'It's Pretty Incredible," *The Knoxville News-Sentinel*, June 9, 2001.

57 the "best player in the South,": "Holly Warlick," *Tennessee Circle of Influence: 2009-10 Lady Vol Basketball*, p. 27, http://www.utladyvols.com/sports/w-baskbl/spec-rel/tennw-w-baskbl-mg2008.html, April 2, 2010.

57 She broke a wrist . . . her roommate was murdered. Strange, "'It's Pretty Incredible.'"

57 I was just in the right place at the right time.: Strange, "'It's Pretty Incredible.'"

58 also left the players and the . . . lasted only 48 hours,: Bebb, p. 320.

58 UT had never known tragedy of such magnitude.: Bebb, p. 320.

58 "You just don't play . . . them and respect them.": Bebb, pp. 320, 322.

58 Houston graciously offered . . . had happened that week.": Bebb, p. 322.

58 The Tennessee players responded . . . them together as a team.: John Shearer, "Memories: 1965 UT Football Team, Coach Bill Majors," *The Chattanoogan. com*, Dec. 5, 2005, http://www.chattanoogan.com/articles/article_76809.asp, April 20, 2010.

59 "the only giveaway that he's . . . being a regular student.": Mike Griffith, "Hometown Hero," *The Knoxville News-Sentinel*, Aug. 31, 2000.

59 "Growing up we had hogs . . . store my parents owned.": Griffith.

59 "I told him that . . . All-American next week.": Griffith.

60 He started out life on . . . indoor plumbing for the first time.: West, *Legends of the Tennessee Vols*, p. 18.

60 He once thought he had . . . paid him for odd jobs.: West, *Legends of the Tennessee Vols*, p. 20.

61 His roommate, J.D. Byington, . . . found the incriminating matches.": West, *Tales of the Tennessee Vols*, p. 145.

61 and hauled Byington away. . . . to pay for the damages. West, *Tales of the Tennessee Vols*, p. 146.

62 "rocks constantly worked[ed] up . . . one side of the field.": Barry Parker and Robin Hood, *Neyland: Life of a Stadium*

	(Chattanooga: Parker Hood Press, Inc., 2000), pp. 3-4.
62	In 1919, Col. W.S. . . . maiden name was Watkins.: Parker & Hood, p. 4.
62	"an unmarked, ungraded expanse . . . resembling playing conditions.: Parker & Hood, p. 5.
62	"Fans are tired of seeing . . . in a sea of mud.": Parker & Hood, p. 7.
62	Before the 1926 season, . . . a turtle-back shape: Parker & Hood, p. 8.
62	Making a field of . . . department's laundry bill.: Parker & Hood, p. 14.
63	Let's get a good one.": Mike Strange, "Tide Can't Catch Vols," *The Knoxville News-Sentinel*, Oct. 25, 1998.
63	"I knew momentum was kind of shifting their way,": Strange, "Tide Can't Catch Vols."
63	"they got a great one." . . . a drink of water,": Strange, "Tide Can't Catch Vols."
64	a "hot young coach . . . about the players returning.": Mike Strange, "DeVoe Was Able to Build Instant Winner," *The Knoxville News-Sentinel*, Jan. 4, 2009.
65	"the best player I ever saw.": West, *Legends of the Tennessee Vols*, p. 29.
65	A Tennessee high school . . . all five for touchdowns.": West, *Legends of the Tennessee Vols*, pp. 29, 31.
65	The opening kickoff "would go . . . me and the goalline.": West, *Legends of the Tennessee Vols*, p. 31.
65	I caught it and took off like a jackrabbit.: West, *Legends of the Tennessee Vols*, p. 31.
66	"conducted a football revival . . . as they had once been.: West, *Legends of the Tennessee Vols*, p. 121.
66	"was a resounding six-year success.": West, *Legends of the Tennessee Vols*, p. 121.
66	He tried to keep his decision . . . before he officially resigned.": West, *Legends of the Tennessee Vols*, p. 125.
66	"It was not a picnic in the park.: West, *Legends of the Tennessee Vols*, pp. 126-27.
66	Revenge was taken." . . . Dickey tipped his cap": West, *Legends of the Tennessee Vols*, p. 126.
67	Early in her career, Summitt . . . she would retire.: Chuck Cavalaris, "Lady Vol Report," *The Knoxville News-Sentinel*, April 8, 2007.
67	pundits considered the most talented team in the country.: Ross, p. 109.
67	"the quintessential game of [her] sterling career.": Ross, p. 109.
67	She had a great . . . at Tennessee four years.": Cavalaris.
68	The noise "made it hard . . . little time for an audible,: Gary Lundy, "Florida Felt 5 Turnovers Contributed to Its Demise," *The Knoxville News-Sentinel*, Sept. 20, 1998.
68	They're not going to beat . . . make a lot of noise.: Warner, p. 236.
69	John Gordy's mom was at the game, . . . a couple of defenders with him.: West, *Tales of the Tennessee Vols*, p. 242.
70	his prize recruits of . . . wanted to go to Kansas.": Moore, *Hoop Tales: Tennessee Volunteers Men's Basketball*, p. 176.
70	His first problem was the . . . Two players left.: Moore, *Hoop Tales: Tennessee Volunteers Men's Basketball*, p. 178.
70	He went to Harris' home . . . and do some things.'": Moore, *Hoop Tales: Tennessee Volunteers Men's Basketball,"* pp. 178, 180.
70	I have no regrets . . . regarding my basketball career.: "Tony Harris Has No Regrets, Want [*sic*] Degree," *The Knoxville News-Sentinel*, Dec. 9, 2007.

71   he seriously considered only . . . recruit them for Georgia Tech.": Manning and Harris, p. 177.

71   "it was the first time . . . it was 60 degrees,": Mike London, "Friday Night Legends: Snapping Back with Stanback," *salisburypost.com*, Nov. 7, 2008, http://www.salisburypost.com/Sports/110708-london-s-legend, April 21, 2010.

71   "I don't mind playing . . . as a regular thing.: Manning and Harris, p. 177.

71   while he was in Knoxville, . . . who would become his wife.: London.

72   "I never thought we'd lose this game.": Mike Strange, "Marathon Men," *The Knoxville News-Sentinel*, Oct. 26, 2003.

72   "all of a sudden a thriller broke out.": Strange, "Marathon Men."

72   To me, religion -- faith -- is the only real thing in life.: Jim & Julie S. Bettinger, *The Book of Bowden* (Nashville: TowleHouse Publishing, 2001), p. 44.

73   As long as Tennessee plays . . . battle with Georgia Tech.": Bebb, p. 270.

73   "the greatest football game I ever saw.": Bebb, p. 271.

73   a later poll selected it . . . Ohio State and Notre Dame).: Bebb, p. 270.

73   Bobby Dodd had aleady said . . . the finest team he had ever had.: Bebb, p. 270.

73   "Every play bore the weight of life and death.": Bebb, p. 273.

73   "gave inches where yards . . . where touchdowns were necessary.": Bebb, p. 271.

74   "I love teeing off first, . . . We were saying, 'Yeah, whatever.'": Dan Fleser, "Smith Likes Hitting First," *The Knoxville News-Sentinel*, April 14, 2006.

75   the game had neither huddles . . . desire for further combat.": Bebb, p. 38.

75   In 1899, for instance, . . . keep the football team alive.: Bebb, pp. 35-36.

75   The 1902 Vanderbilt game . . . the game was $42.35.: Bebb, p. 37.

75   The players wore jerseys, . . . of different colors.: Bebb, p. 37.

75   If a player had $1.25, . . . the shins and elbows.: Bebb, pp. 37-38.

75   Equipment in the way of . . . Scrubs furnished their own.: Bebb, p. 38.

76   the coach of Knoxville's South . . . and I won the job.": Mike Strange, "Colquitt Went from Department Store to UT Punter in 1975," *GoVolsXtra. com*, July 3, 2009, http://www.govolsxtra.com/news/2009/jul/03/just-for-kicks/, March 12, 2010.

76   After graduation in 1972, . . . said come on down.: Glier, p. 130.

76   He attempted to punt . . . hit my face mask.": Glier, p. 132.

76   I feel like I've handed down a business to my sons.: Strange, "Colquitt Went from Department Store."

77   after being told . . . to play in the SEC.: "Reliving the Tennessee Volunteers 2005 Football Season, *viewfromrockytop.com*, July 20, 2008, http://www.view fromrockytop.com/category/tennessee-volunteer-football/players/rick-clausen, April 21, 2010.

77   The week of the LSU game . . . good enough to start.: Mark Burgess, "Clausen Writes a Storybook Finish," *The Knoxville News-Sentinel*, Sept. 27, 2005.

77   "one of the greatest comebacks in UT football history.": "Reliving the Tennessee Volunteers 2005 Football Season."

77   It was a tough week . . . know what will happen.: Burgess.

78   "The game was won and lost on the boards,": Drew Edwards, "Second-Half Rebounds Prove Heroic Like Hopson," *UTSPORTS.COM*, Jan. 31, 2010, http://www.utsports.com/sports/m-baskbl/spec-rel/013110aaa.html, April 23, 2010.

78	it wasn't even a fair fight . . . going to be a battle.: Edwards.
78	"Win this for us." Hopson dutifully replied, 'Yes, sir.": Edwards
78	"When I got the ball, . . . I knew it went in.": Edwards.
79	"There was nothing attractive . . . an intense desire to play.": Cawood, p. 5.
79	Alabama had recorded . . . spectators' car headlights.: Cawood, pp. 5-6.
79	"the most talked-about . . . game in Tennessee's history.": Bebb, p. 99.
79	"Next year" was here at last.: Bebb, p. 103.
80	before the 1946 game at . . . expressions on their faces.": West, *Legends of the Tennessee Vols*, p. 5.
80	tailback Pat Shires missed . . . for his team to hear: West, *Legends of the Tennessee Vols*, p. 5.
80	"Don't worry about that . . . down here to tie.": Gilbert, p.p. 186-87.
80	When this game's over . . . the 'Tennessee Waltz.': Gilbert, p. 186.
81	"Except for participating in . . . "a virtual stranger,": Moore, *Hoop Tales: Tennessee Lady Volunteers*, p. 42.
81	"a motley crew of sixty walk-on candidates": Moore, *Hoop Tales: Tennessee Lady Volunteers*, p. 41.
81	She managed to make it . . . play pattern or freelance?": Moore, *Hoop Tales: Tennessee Lady Volunteers*, p. 41.
81	Hutson had no idea . . . you'll be coaching women's basketball.": Moore, *Hoop Tales: Tennessee Lady Volunteers*, p. 42.
81	The job was so incidental . . . or a handshake.: Moore, *Hoop Tales: Tennessee Lady Volunteers*, p. 43.
81	She embarked on a crash . . . a player named Pat Head.: Moore, *Hoop Tales: Tennessee Lady Volunteers*, p. 44.
82	"arguably the most sought-after athlete in America.": Moore, *Stadium Stories*, p. 104.
82	When his mother nixed . . . he decided on football.: Moore, *Stadium Stories*, p. 106.
82	On a recruiting visit, . . . "We're not ready for this.": Glier, p. 111.
82	"What Coach Bryant did . . . a 17-year-old kid?": Glier, p. 111.
82	"told me if I was . . . I could play quarterback.": Glier, p. 109.
82	Being a Volunteer is about . . . later when you left.: Glier, p. 113.
83	"the game appeared to be a colossal mismatch.": Moore, *Stadium Stories*, p. 115.
83	"mind-boggling": Moore, *Stadium Stories*, p. 114.
83	This evening belonged . . . band of Volunteers.: Moore, *Stadium Stories*, p. 116.
84	Her heftiest budget for the basketball team was $500.: Moore, *Hoop Tales: Tennessee Lady Volunteers*, p. 20.
84	The teams comprised primarily . . . and staying in dorms.: Schriver, p. xxvi.
84	Once as awards for . . . a hundred for a dollar,": Moore, *Hoop Tales: Tennessee Lady Volunteers*, p. 18.
84	I knew what was coming.: Moore, *Hoop Tales: Tennessee Lady Volunteers*, p. 18.
85	UT line coach Ray Trail . . . a good man, a good Christian.": West, *Legends of the Tennessee Vols*, p. 75.
85	most of all he liked . . . he and teammates did.": West, *Legends of the Tennessee Vols*, p. 77.
85	What the heck is a Bengal?: West, *Legends of the Tennessee Vols*, p. 76.
86	"a bona fide flake." . . . and clowned constantly." Moore, *Hoop Tales: Tennessee Volunteers Men's Basketball*, p. 181.

86	"all-out effort, coupled with . . . bite 'em or something.'": Moore, *Hoop Tales: Tennessee Volunteers Men's Basketball*, p. 185.
86	He snared an offensive . . . "brutality of the assault,": Moore, *Hoop Tales: Tennessee Volunteers Men's Basketball*, p. 185.
86	"apparently blessed with miraculous . . . typically uninhibited celebration.": Moore, *Hoop Tales: Tennessee Volunteers Men's Basketball*, p. 185.
86	I was working on my Oscar performance for later this year.: Moore, *Hoop Tales: Tennessee Volunteers Men's Basketball*, p. 185.
87	A 13-year-old soccer player . . . in the stands that night.: Manning and Harris, p. 46.
87	Duncan and his family . . . missionary work in Kenya: Manning and Harris, p. 45.
87	What impressed young Duncan . . . good on his kicks.: Manning and Harris, p. 46.
87	"I bet I can . . . kicking for the Vols.": Manning and Harris, p. 48.
87	He declared he was staying . . . stay together as a family.": Manning and Harris, pp. 45-46.
87	the teenager realized God . . . in service as a missionary.: Manning and Harris, p. 48.
87	He wrote UT coach . . . in August of 1976: Manning and Harris, p. 49.
88	He had gained some fame . . . catapulted him over the line.: Bebb, p. 64.
88	In the spring, that . . . 30,000 Tennessee men responded.: Bebb, p. 70.
88	One of the admirers . . . that it will stick.: Bebb, p. 70.
89	she "had a lackadaisical attitude . . . everything would be fine.": Ross, p. 84.
89	Charles skipped a class . . . child and family studies.: Ross, p. 84.
89	The lessons learned on . . . to the field of life.: Warner, p. 224.
90	The week before the Bama . . . apt the Moses image was: Phillip Fulmer with Jeff Hagood, *A Perfect Season* (Nashville: Rutledge Hill Press, 1999) p. 96.
90	Fulmer admitted to himself . . . went everywhere after that.: Fulmer with Hagood, p. 97.
90	"One player carried it . . . they would win them all.: Fulmer with Hagood, p. 98.
90	Is this corny or what?: Fulmer with Hagood, p. 97.

BIBLIOGRAPHY

Adams, John. "For 11 Minutes, It was Like Old Times for UT's Milligan." *The Knoxville News-Sentinel*. 23 Feb. 1998.

---. "From the Mean Streets to Monster Hits -- Cover Story: Kevin Burnett." *The Knoxville News-Sentinel*. 17 Aug. 2003.

---. "Mears 'Lived for a Good Battle.'" *The Knoxville News-Sentinel*. 12 June 2007.

---. "Of Such Wins Are Championships Made." *The Knoxville News-Sentinel*. 15 Nov. 1998.

Balloch, Jim. "Summitt Shoots for Record Book: Lady Vol Coach's Legendary Success Only Hinted at Early on, Former Players Say." *The Knoxville News-Sentinel*. 22 March 2005.

Bebb, Russ. *The Big Orange: A Story of Tennessee Football*. Huntsville, AL: The Strode Publishers, 1973.

Bettinger, Jim & Julie S. *The Book of Bowden*. Nashville: TowleHouse Publishing, 2001.

Browning, Al. *Third Saturday in October: The Game-by-Game Story of the South's Most Intense Football Rivalry*. Nashville: Cumberland House, 2001.

Burgess, Mark. "Clausen Writes a Storybook Finish for UT; Backup QB Defeats Former Teammates." *The Knoxville News-Sentinel*. 27 Sept. 2005.

Cavalaris, Chuck. "Lady Vol Report." *The Knoxville News-Sentinel*. 8 April 2007.

Cawood, Chris. *Legacy of the Swamp Rat: Tennessee Quarterbacks Who Just Said No to Alabama*. Kingston, TN: Magnolia Hill Press, 1994.

Climer, David. "Tennessee's J.P. Prince Defends Final Play Against Ohio State as Just a 'Clean Block.'" *The Tennessean*. 27 March 2010. http://pqasb.pqarchiver.com/tennessean/advancedsearch.html.

---. "Vols Have Earned Elite Status." *The Tennessean*. 27 March 2010. http://pqasb.pqarchiver.com/tennessean/advancedsearch.html.

Dahlberg, Bruce T. "Anger." *The Interpreter's Dictionary of the Bible*. Nashville: Abingdon Press, 1962. Vol. 1. 135-37.

Edwards, Drew. "Second-Half Rebounds Prove Heroic Like Hopson." *UTSPORTS.COM*. 31 Jan. 2010. http://www.utsports.com/sports/m-baskbl/spec-rel/013110aaa.html.

Fleser, Dan. "Coaching Legend Still Grateful UT took a Chance." *The Knoxville News-Sentinel*. 23 March 2005.

---. "Smith Likes Hitting First . . . Long; Freshman Golfer Plays Key Role for Lady Vols." *The Knoxville News-Sentinel*. 14 April 2006.

Fulmer, Phillip with Jeff Hagood. *A Perfect Season*. Nashville: Rutledge Hill Press, 1999.

Gilbert, Bob. *Neyland: The Gridiron General*. Savannah: Golden Coast Publishing Company, 1990.

Glier, Ray. *What It Means to Be a Volunteer: Phillip Fulmer and Tennessee's Greatest Players*. Chicago: Triumph Books, 2008.

Griffith, Mike. "Hometown Hero: Finlayson the Farmer Still Producing as UT Tight End." *The Knoxville News-Sentinel*. 31 Aug. 2000.

"Holly Warlick: 25th Season at Tennessee." *Tennessee Circle of Influence: 2009-10 Lady Vol Basketball.* 26-27. http://www.utladyvols.com/sports/w-baskbl/spec-rel/tennw-w-baskbl-mg2008.html.

"Jack Reynolds (American football)." *Wikipedia, the free encyclopedia.* http://en.wikipedia.org/wiki/Jack_Reynolds_(American_Football).

Julian, Roland. "Widseth's Name, Numbers Scary." *GoVolsXtra.* 5 Jan. 2008. http://www.govolsxtra.com/news/2008/jan05/widseths-name-numbers-scary/.

Kenner, Randy. "Never Too Late for UT Athletes to Graduate; Stowell Earns Degree 12 Years After Ending His Vol Football Career." *The Knoxville News-Sentinel.* 11 Dec. 2004.

London, Mike. "Friday Night Legends: Snapping Back with Stanback." *salisburypost.com.* 7 Nov. 2008. http://www.salisburypost.com/Sports/110708-london-s-legend.

Lundy, Gary. "Florida Felt 5 Turnovers Contributed to Its Demise." *The Knoxville News-Sentinel.* 20 Sept. 1998.

---. "Vols Adapt to Late-Night Kickoff in Different Ways." *The Knoxville News-Sentinel.* 15 Oct. 2004.

---. "Vols Hog the Glory: Arkansas Fumble Aids UT's Rally." *The Knoxville News-Sentinel.* 15 Nov. 1998.

MacArthur, John. *Twelve Ordinary Men* (Nashville: W Publishing Group, 2002).

Manning, Gus and Haywood Harris. *Once a Vol, Always a Vol! The Proud Men of the Volunteer Nation.* Champaign, IL: Sports Publishing L.L.C., 2006.

Mattingly, Tom. "Sines Did Mears One Better, Scheduled Doubleheader." *The Knoxville News-Sentinel.* 7 Dec. 2008.

Minear, P.S. "Hope." *The Interpreter's Dictionary of the Bible.* Vol. 2: E-J. Nashville, Abingdon Press, 1990. 640-43.

Moore, Randy. *Hoop Tales: Tennessee Lady Volunteers.* Guilford, CN: The Globe Pequot Press, 2005.

---. *Hoop Tales: Tennessee Volunteers Men's Basketball.* Guilford, CN: The Globe Pequot Press, 2005.

---. *Stadium Stories: Tennessee Volunteers: Colorful Tales of the Orange and White.* Guilford, CN: The Globe Pequot Press, 2004.

Parker, Barry and Robin Hood. *Neyland: Life of a Stadium.* Chattanooga: Parker Hood Press, Inc., 2000.

"Reliving the Tennessee Volunteers 2005 Football Season: Part 4, LSU and the Rally in the Valley." *viewfromrockytop.com.* 20 July 2008. http://www.viewfromrockytop.com/category/tennessee-volunteer-football/players/rick-clausen.

Ross, Alan. *Seven: The National Championship Teams of the Tennessee Lady Vols.* Nashville: Cumberland House, 2007.

Schriver, Debby. *In the Footsteps of Champions: The University of Tennessee Lady Volunteers, the First Three Decades.* Nashville: The University of Tennessee Press, 2008.

Shearer, John. "Memories: 1965 UT Football Team, Coach Bill Majors." *The Chattanoogan.com.* 5 Dec. 2005. http://www.

TENNESSEE

chattanoogan.com/articles/article/_76809.asp.

Staples, Andy." Dooley Aiming to Salvage Messy Situation, Earn Vols' Respect." *Sports Illustrated*. 16 April 2010. http://sportsillustrated.cnn.com/2010/ writers/andy_staples/04/16/tennessee-dooley/index.html.

Strange, Mike. "'28 Vols Ended Domination by Beating Commodores." *The Knoxville News-Sentinel*. 23 Nov. 2000.

---. "Colquitt Went from Department Store to UT Punter in 1975." *GoVolsXtra. com*. 3 July 2009. http://www.govolsextra.com/news/2009/jul/03/just-for-kicks/.

---. "Denney Still Recalls How UT Faked out Syracuse in '66." *The Knoxville News-Sentinel*. 3 Sept. 1998.

---. "DeVoe Was Able to Build Instant Winner." *The Knoxville News-Sentinel*. 20 Jan. 2009.

---. "In '50 Game, Vols Put Freeze on Wildcats' Dreams of Title." *The Knoxville News-Sentinel*. 19 Nov. 1998.

---. "'It's Pretty Incredible': Warlick at Home in Hall." *The Knoxville News-Sentinel*. 9 June 2001.

---. "Learning on the Run: Ritzmann Fitting in with Vols." *The Knoxville News-Sentinel*. 21 Sept. 2001.

---. "Marathon Men: Clausen Leads UT Past Alabama in Five OTs, 51-43." *The Knoxville News Sentinel*. 26 Oct. 2003.

---. "Night Crawler: Temple Set Stage in Knoxville for Time Clock." *The Knoxville News-Sentinel*. 8 Nov. 2007.

---. "Robinson a Pioneer: First UT Black on Court of Orange and White." *The Knoxville News-Sentinel*. 28 Feb. 2006.

---. "Tide Can't Catch Vols -- UT: four in a Row over Bama." *The Knoxville News-Sentinel*. 25 Oct. 1998.

---. "Vols' 1980 Victory against Auburn Came from Nowhere." *The Knoxville News-Sentinel*. 1 Oct. 1998.

---. "Vols' Sub-Flub Pays Off: A Little Luck Helps Fulmer Get 100th Win." *The Knoxville News-Sentinel*. 3 Nov. 2002.

Summitt, Pat with Sally Jenkins. *Raise the Roof: The Inspiring Inside Story of the Tennessee Lady Vols' Undefeated 1997-98 Season*. New York: Broadway Books, 1998.

"Tony Harris Has No Regrets, Want [sic] Degree." *The Knoxville News-Sentinel*. Dec. 9, 2007.

Venable, Sam. "Both Soared to Record Heights." *The Knoxville News-Sentinel*. 24 March 2005.

"Vols Mourn Loss of Former All-America Tight End Denney." UTSPORTS.COM. 22 Jan. 2009. http://www.utsports.com/sports/m-footbl/spec-rel/012209aaa. html.

Warner, Chris. *SEC Sports Quotes*. Baton Rouge: CEW Enterprises, 2002.

West, Marvin. *Legends of the Tennessee Vols*. Champaign, IL: Sports Publishing L.L.C., 2005.

---. *Tales of the Tennessee Vols*. Champaign, ILL: Sports Publishing L.L.C., 2001.

VOLUNTEERS

INDEX
(LAST NAME, DEVOTION DAY NUMBER)

197